Local Lending

Goth

Gothic Whitby

Colin Waters

The
History
Press

Frontispiece: St Oswald's Church, Lythe.

First published 2009
Reprinted 2014

The History Press
The Mill, Brimscombe Port
Stroud, Gloucestershire, GL5 2QG
www.thehistorypress.co.uk

British Library Cataloguing in Publication Data.
A catalogue record for this book is available from the British Library.

ISBN 978 0 7524 5291 3

Typesetting and origination by The History Press
Printed and bound in Great Britain by
Marston Book Services Limited, Oxfordshire

Contents

CHAPTER ONE

In Dracula's Footsteps

Count Dracula in Fact and Fiction

I remember how much the Dailygraph and The Whitby Gazette, of which I had made cuttings, had helped us to understand the terrible events at Whitby when Count Dracula landed.

(Mina Harker's journal)

When Abraham Stoker came to Whitby in 1890, on holiday with his family, he could have had no way of knowing that his stay in the town would inspire him to write a Gothic literary masterpiece. Since its publication, his novel *Dracula*, originally intended to be published as *The Un-Dead*, has been translated into numerous languages and has been portrayed in every media form possible, including pantomime, stage shows, television series, radio plays – and of course films, commencing with the Gothic classic *Nosferatu*, starring Max Shrecke, in 1922. The word 'Nosferatu' translates in Latin as *nos*, we, *fera*, wild animal, and *tu*, you (roughly speaking, 'we are all wild animals', though there have been various other interpretations and explanations).

The word appears in *Dracula* on a number of occasions, including one entry that gives its own ungrammatical explanation: 'The nosferatu do not die like the bee when he stings once. He is only stronger, and being stronger, have yet more power to work evil.'

It has been claimed that Bram Stoker stayed at a number of boarding houses in the town over the years; however, it is known for certain that he spent at least some of his early vacations at the home of seaside landlady Fanny Harker and her husband William: indeed, the Harker and the Stoker families became firm friends, so much so that he promised to use their surname and address in his future novel. True to his word, their home at 7 Royal Crescent Avenue (now Crescent Avenue) appeared in the story as '7 The Crescent', and the Harker name became an integral part of the Dracula story.

The Real Dracula

This use of real names, places and people was not unusual in Stoker's novels, and *Dracula* proved no exception. For instance, Professor Vambery of the Budapest University of Languages is said to have inspired the character of Professor Van Helsing, whilst it is widely accepted that the main character, Dracula, is based on Count Vladimir Tepes (pronounced Tse-pesh), whose name is often contracted to 'Vlad Drac III'.

The surname Tepes translates as 'Impaler', and refers to the tyrant's favourite method of punishing prisoners and law-breakers. Vlad III was, like his father before him, a member of an elite group of European Catholic princes who had vowed to defend Europe against the onslaught of the Ottaman Turks. The group was known as the Order of the Dragon. The Romanian word for dragon (and incidentally, also the word for Devil) is *drac*, whilst the suffix *ula* means 'son of'. Thus the name Dracula actually means 'son of the dragon' as well as 'son of the Devil', depending on the user's point of view.

One story that has survived to illustrate the historical Drac III's reputation for total intolerance of law breaking amongst his subjects concerns a solid gold cup that he ordered should be secretly laced with poisoned wine. In the dead of night the cup was placed in the central square of the town of Tirgoviste to tempt thieves. Such was the fear of retribution from Vlad Drac that it is said that not a single person attempted to steal the cup or even tried to drink from it. This episode illustrates well the ruler's disturbed and distinctively cruel nature, a fact that has been confirmed in both Russian and German documents. In one notable case, diplomats from both countries had arrived at Vlad's court for a political meeting. Despite being titled Prince, the envoys did not recognise him as a true Royal sovereign and refused to remove their hats in his presence as instructed. The outraged Vlad is said to have flown into a rage at this snub and ordered that their hats should be nailed to their heads as a demonstration of his disapproval, a punishment that was duly carried out.

The feared leader's reign of terror ended with his death in December 1476, by which time he was considered a tyrant by some and a religious saviour by others. Despite his evil deeds, his body was buried within the grounds of Snagov monastery, where it lay undisturbed for about three years until officials ordered his remains to be disinterred. Strangely, when his coffin was opened it was found to be completely empty, a sign for some that he was a kind of Messiah and had risen from the dead and ascended to heaven. The superstitious peasant population of Transylvania and Wallachia, however, was now convinced that Dracula had become a vampire. As such, his undead corpse was destined to travel the earth for eternity, seeking out the innocent victims in order to feed the Count's blood lust.

Though his descendants are poorly documented, the real-life Dracula's bloodline has certainly continued through to modern times. Following her death in Paris aged seventy-six on 14 May 1997, newspapers revealed that the Romanian Princess Catherine Caradja, otherwise known as Caradja-Kretzulesco, was in fact a direct descendent of Prince Vlad the Impaler. The princess had formerly fled from Bucharest to France to escape Communist rule in 1947. In contrast to her ancestor's life of evil, she had become an active charity worker in her later years, collecting money in aid of Romanian citizens after the country's political overthrow in 1989.

Stoker's Dracula

Bram Stoker, though a well-balanced and pleasant individual with a definite sense of humour, was said to be unavoidably attracted to the study of 'all things dark'. It has been acknowledged that as well as being a Freemason he was almost certainly a member of the Golden Dawn, an influential occult society that attracted Victorian academics, spies, university professors and diplomats who, it is said, gathered in secret to discuss and explore a wide range of mystical and taboo subjects.

It is also said that before writing his novel, Stoker spent seven years studying European folklore, especially the vampire stories from the region of Transylvania, having had his interest sparked by an 1885 essay entitled 'Transylvania Superstitions' written by Emily Gerard, the wife of the influential Chevalier Miecislas de Laszowski. Laszowski was a cavalry officer who, together with his wife, had been stationed in the Transylvanian town of Temesvar (now Timisoara, Romania). Another of Stoker's associates who influenced his interest in vampires was Arminius Vambery, a Hungarian writer and traveller who was also a keen collector of superstitions and legends from the Baltic regions.

Because of these interests, there is no doubt that Stoker delighted in the Gothic, mysterious and historic aspects of Whitby, and indeed two real-life maritime incidents were instrumental in the town becoming a key part of the story. One involved a mysterious and apparently unmanned ship that sailed out of the fog near Whitby Harbour entrance and rammed a local fishing vessel, tipping its crew into the water. The ship then, despite the desperate cries of the distressed crew, sailed off into the mist, never to be seen again. The second real-life incident to have an influence on the story of *Dracula* was the wrecking of a Russian vessel, the *Dmitri* of Narva, in October 1885. It was carrying sand along the north-east coast and got into difficulty in atrocious weather. As it started to take in water its cargo of sand became unstable: the vessel limped through the harbour mouth at Whitby and was wrecked upon Tate Hill beach. In true form, Stoker slightly disguised the incident, transforming the *Dmitri* into the *Demeter* and giving its home port as Varna (an anagram of the real port of Navra.)

Bram Stoker knew that both the names 'Demeter' and 'Dmitri' had virtually the same meaning. 'Dimitri' was the Russian version of the Greek Demeter and as such is the equivalent of the British Earth Mother goddess. To the Romans she was known as Ceres, whilst the Celtic tribes knew her as Gaia or Mother Earth, the primeval Mother goddess of all goddesses. The fifty boxes of loam carried upon the Demeter, which were also no doubt meant to symbolically convey the same 'earth' message, were in the story consigned to Mr Billington the solicitor at 7 The Crescent before finally being delivered to Carfax House near Purfleet. Stoker is believed to have based his, or rather his character Jonathan Harker's, description of Carfax House ('close to an old chapel or church') on 'Purfleet House', which was built there in 1791 by Samuel Whitbread, the brewer, together with a detached chapel for the 'ease of use of his family'.

Whitby's Place in the Novel

The first brief mention of Whitby occurs in chapter two of Jonathan Harker's diary, where it is described as being ringed on a map. It next appears in chapter three, where the address '7 The Crescent' is given as the office of Samuel Billington. Whitby fully enters the story in chapter six where an evocative and accurate description of the town in Victorian times is given:

> Right over the town is the ruin of Whitby Abbey, which was sacked by the Danes, and which is the scene of part of 'Marmion,' where the girl was built up in the wall. It is a most noble ruin, of immense size, and full of beautiful and romantic bits. There is a legend that a white lady is seen in one of the windows. Between it and the town there is another church, the parish one, round which is a big graveyard, all full of tombstones. This is to my mind the nicest spot in Whitby, for it lies right over the town, and has a full view of the harbour and all up the bay to where the headland called Kettleness stretches out into the sea. It descends so steeply over the harbour that part of the bank has fallen away, and some of the graves have been destroyed. In one place part of the stonework of the graves stretches out over the sandy pathway far below. There are walks, with seats beside them, through the churchyard, and people go and sit there all day long looking at the beautiful view and enjoying the breeze.

It would take many pages to recount all of the descriptions of Whitby given by Stoker in the novel, but those who have not read the book for themselves could do no better than to spend a while reading through its pages, admiring its accuracy and perhaps trying to decipher some of the mystic, symbolic or veiled references that the author used throughout the story.

Influential characters that appear in the pages of the book may well have been based on Stoker's acquaintances in Whitby. Like the Harkers, it is at least possible that whilst sharing a glass of sherry with the author at the local Freemason's Lodge, his acquaintances had been promised an 'appearance' in the forthcoming Whitby novel. Amongst these characters is Doctor Seward, who, it has been speculated, is a veiled reference to a Doctor Stewart who had a surgery at 2 Skinner Street, not far from Stoker's lodging in 1890. A second local businessman, Mr Charles Buchanan, solicitor of Crescent Place, who also lived nearby and had offices at Baxtergate, may well have been the model for the fictitious solicitor Samuel F. Billington.

There have been many attempts by academics to decipher various aspects of the story, to look for hidden meanings, or to link real-life people to the characters that appear in the book. One character, Mr Swales (a common local fishing family name), appears a number of times in Mina Murray's journal. A Mrs Swales is known to have run another seaside guesthouse at that time at 2 East Crescent. Could it be that Stoker had stayed there at some time but that he had not had the best of relations with her or her husband? We are told in Mina Murray's journal for the 10 August that the grumpy old character Mr Swales:

> ...was found dead this morning on our seat, his neck being broken. He had evidently, as the doctor said, fallen back in the seat in some sort of fright, for there was a look of fear and horror on his face that the men said made them shudder. Poor dear old man!

CHAPTER TWO

Gone But Not Forgotten

A Tour of St Mary's Graveyard

Finger rings made of lead, taken from a coffin, were worn as a cure for cramp.

(Whitby Past & Present, 1897)

Though the seat on which Mr Swales met his untimely end will have long decayed, other seats have been placed at various viewpoints along the cliff-top path. Overlooked by the weathered gargoyles on the old church tower, they continue to be used today by countless visitors who climb the 199 stone steps to look out over the town and to take in the brooding atmosphere of the churchyard, or perhaps to read the weathered inscriptions on the tombstones whilst contemplating the meaning of life and death. As if to remind them of their fragile earthly existence, an ancient weathered sundial dating from 1737, set high above the south side of the church wall, proclaims the profound message 'Our Days Pass Like A Shadow'.

The ancient cemetery still stands very much as Stoker would have found it, and St Mary's Church and graveyard remain as timeless as ever, despite the cliff edge having fallen away over the years (causing graves to be removed when they threatened to fall over the edge). Bats still fly around the area

The fading ancient sundial on the wall of the parish church predates the clock faces on the church tower by hundreds of years.

at night, and crows; jackdaws and ravens can often be seen perching upon the tops of the ancient gravestones and gargoyles as if placed there by some Gothically-minded film director. The tombstones have sadly deteriorated (having been weathered away by the constant biting wind and squally weather that blows off the North Sea). Even in recent years the path leading along the northern cliff edge has been walled off due to cliff erosion and yet further graves have had to be rescued from falling over the cliff. Among these are victims of the 1861 lifeboat disaster: their tombstones now rest casually against the southern wall of the church beneath the sundial.

Visitors to the town who seek Dracula's grave are constantly directed to this churchyard by local shopkeepers who, with tongue firmly in cheek, give their own account of where to find his final place of rest. Many are told to look out for the small railed-off area to the south-east of the church and are assured that one or other of these gravestones marks the true resting place of the vampire. In reality, this patch mainly serves as the burial place of past clergymen, though there are a number of interesting things to look out for.

For well over a century local children have been told by their parents that the nursery characters Tom Thumb and Humpty Dumpty are buried in this little plot. Even disbelieving children have eventually become convinced of the story when confronted by the 'evidence' in the form of a tiny gravestone,

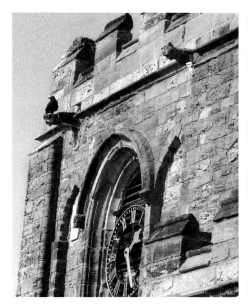

A bird rests on one of the ancient gargoyles. Below it, on the base of the arch over the clock, can be seen two ancient carved faces.

Rescued from falling over the cliff edge: the tombstone of John Storr, coxswain of the ill-fated lifeboat which sank (with the loss of twelve lives) in the maritime disaster of February 1861.

jammed between two larger gravestones (probably the grave of a child) and the unusual flat, oval gravestone nearby where, they are assured, the broken pieces of Humpty Dumpty were finally laid to rest. Of more interest to adults is the strange Huntrodds' epitaph. This unobtrusive but unusual grave is tucked away in a small archway below steps in the corner of this enclosed plot. Close to the grave can be seen an ancient Saxon doorway flanked by a pair of worn carved stone heads. The inscription on the Huntrodds' epitaph is now largely worn away, but it has been reproduced on a plaque above the grave.

This odd memorial inscription has attracted the interest of a number of amateur cryptologists who are convinced that it holds some hidden message. Many have tried to find some sort of code or meaning to the words, dates, spacing and odd punctuation. Others have been puzzled by the words, '...so fit a match; surely could never be...', and are convinced that this is evidence that the story cannot be true. So far nobody has managed to solve the conundrum, if indeed one exists at all, though the Huntrodds were indeed a local family who attended this church in times past.

This same railed-off section of the graveyard also contains one of Whitby's oldest tombstones that can still be read. Though it is heavily worn, when the light is right a faint inscription can be seen whilst standing on the footpath outside the fence. What remains of the inscription appears to read:

According to generations of local children, the remains of Humpty Dumpty lie in this odd-shaped grave.

This tiny gravestone is probably the grave of a child, but many Whitby children once firmly believed it marked Tom Thumb's last resting place.

Hidden away in the corner of the railed off area of Whitby churchyard, many visitors miss the unusual grave of Francis and Mary Huntrodd.

Does the Huntrodd's epitaph, as some believe, contain a hidden cryptic message? If so, no one has yet been able to decipher it.

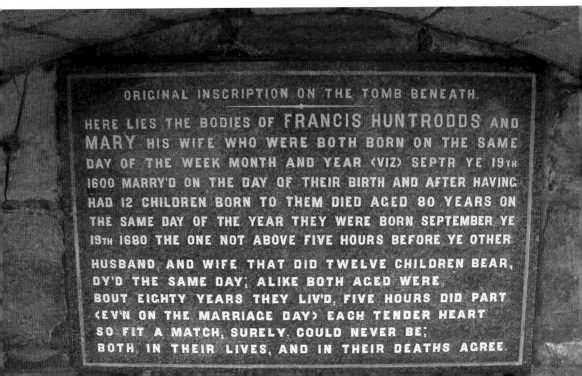

ORIGINAL INSCRIPTION ON THE TOMB BENEATH.

HERE LIES THE BODIES OF FRANCIS HUNTRODDS AND MARY HIS WIFE WHO WERE BOTH BORN ON THE SAME DAY OF THE WEEK MONTH AND YEAR (VIZ) SEPTR YE 19TH 1600 MARRY'D ON THE DAY OF THEIR BIRTH AND AFTER HAVING HAD 12 CHILDREN BORN TO THEM DIED AGED 80 YEARS ON THE SAME DAY OF THE YEAR THEY WERE BORN SEPTEMBER YE 19TH 1680 THE ONE NOT ABOVE FIVE HOURS BEFORE YE OTHER

HUSBAND, AND WIFE THAT DID TWELVE CHILDREN BEAR, DY'D THE SAME DAY; ALIKE BOTH AGED WERE, BOUT EIGHTY YEARS THEY LIV'D, FIVE HOURS DID PART (EV'N ON THE MARRIAGE DAY) EACH TENDER HEART SO FIT A MATCH, SURELY, COULD NEVER BE; BOTH, IN THEIR LIVES, AND IN THEIR DEATHS AGREE.

In memory of Ralph King who departed his life January [...] 1697 aged 38 years. Also [Marian] Dear departed... April... Aged 64 [Jane]...

Nearby and quite close to the churchyard exit gate, on the path leading from this section towards the Abbey Plain, will be found the remaining two of the once three 'Pirates' Graves'. These gravestones are often missed, even by the most ardent reader of inscriptions, as they lie close to the ground and have no writing upon them whatsoever. Their most interesting feature is the carved skull and crossbones to be found on the end of each slab. These odd and somewhat grotesquely carved blocks are in fact the remains of 'table' shaped gravestones. The flat 'table tops' still lie close by but are unreadable. Though it would be nice to think that they mark the tombs of some ancient buccaneers, the truth is more mundane. As Bram Stoker would have been aware, they are in fact the last resting place of Master Freemasons, the skull and crossbone imagery having been borrowed from Masonic third degree symbolism.

The readability of the inscriptions upon most of these ancient tombstones is very variable and depends largely upon both the lighting conditions and the weather. Often writing which is totally unreadable at one time will magically

The so-called 'Pirates' Graves' are situated close to the left-hand side of the path leading towards the Abbey Plain but are often missed by the most enthusiastic of gravestone browsers.

Only two of the three remaining so-called 'Pirates' Graves' remain. They actually serve as the burial place of master masons, the skull and crossbones symbolism being taken directly from third degree master mason imagery.

leap into legibility when the sun is at a certain angle or days of rain have thoroughly soaked the porous sandstone. Those that are decipherable reveal many sad incidences of infant deaths or of master mariners lost at sea. Other inscriptions record sailors who died in foreign waters, never to return to their home town. In effect, they serve as memorials rather than graves, reminding us of the words of old Mr Swales in chapter six of Dracula:

> Why, it's them that, not content with printin' lies on paper an' preachin' them out of pulpits, does want to be cuttin' them on the tombstones. Look here all around you in what airt ye will. All them steans, holdin' up their heads as well as they can out of their pride, is acant, simply tumblin' down with the weight o' the lies wrote on them, 'Here lies the body' or 'Sacred to the memory' wrote on all of them, an' yet in nigh half of them there bean't no bodies at all...

Examples of these kinds of headstones include the two illustrated overleaf; one being a memorial to Thomas Burnett, master mariner, who (together with his crew) was lost on a passage from St Andrews to Whitby on or about the 7 January 1834, and another to one of the children of William and Amelia Brown (buried in Highgate Cemetery, London, in grave No. 282, on 27 August 1848).

It was quite common in Victorian Whitby to erect gravestones to people who were not actual buried there, such as this one to a mariner who was lost at sea and the adjacent stone recording the death of a child who was buried in Highgate Cemetery, London.

A once-renowned uninhabited 'grave' of this type has been lost to the elements, but older residents of the town still speak of an ancient tombstone, now sadly eroded beyond legibility, which bore the ungrammatical and contradictory inscription, 'Here lies the body of Isaac Green whose body was lost at sea and never found.'

Whitby folklore records a number of grim tales of people being buried alive in this cemetery. An old woman named Martha Dryden narrowly escaped this fate. As she lay naked on a kitchen table – her body was about to be washed and 'laid out' in preparation for burial – her rings were removed to be given to her relatives. This latter action brought her out of what had apparently been a coma, and the fortunate old lady fully recovered to live on for many years afterwards. In another case, a man variously said to have the name Hutchinson or Underwood was not so lucky. Sharing a pint in a pub some hours after the funeral, the pall bearers began to worry that the man they had just buried had not been dead, recollecting that the coffin had noisily rocked around as they carried it up the 199 steps. When asked why they had not opened the coffin to check on the man's condition, they all agreed that they had thought about it, but decided that they couldn't do anything about the situation – the reason, they said, being that the lid was already nailed down!

Like all cemeteries, this ancient burial place is a great leveller. It has become the last resting place of people from all aspects of society ranging from ordinary jet workers and fishermen to those who went on to make their mark in life. Records tell us that up to the 1850s there were distinct social divisions in the town and everyone knew their place. This Victorian class structure involved strict social codes which extended even to the ringing of the funeral bell. Those of a certain station were given the conventional dignity of a slow toll, but at the funerals of people from poor families the bell was rung at 'an exceedingly fast pace'.

Whilst touring the cemetery, look out for a modern gravestone marking the burial place of the arctic explorer William Scoresby. Scoresby invented the barrel-shaped crow's nest for sailors, a replica of which stands atop a mast at Dock End, close to the tourist information bureau. The 'gravestone' of local writer Mary Linskill, situated almost opposite to the main church entrance, is another example of the ones referred to by Mr Swales and as such does not actually contain her body. Mary was born in Blackburn's Yard in the upper part of Church Street. The cottage in which she gave birth has now gone, but a plaque marking the site can still be seen in a garden near to the top of the yard steps. No such plaque marks the house in Spring Vale where she died on the 9 April 1891 at the relatively young age of fifty.

A careful search in the far north-east corner of the cemetery will reveal a rare example of a cast-iron tombstone. It is one of the few gravestones in Britain to be made of metal and was produced at the Baxtergate foundry of engineer George Chapman. The memorial stone was actually constructed by him before his death with the intention of eventually marking the grave of himself and his wife, Elizabeth. It was originally painted black and was topped by an urn, also made of iron. The inscription is still readable and serves as a sad reminder of the great infant mortality rate that was prevalent during Victorian times as it records the deaths of the couple's young children, Esther, Edward and John William. George Chapman was one of two iron founders in Whitby in the early 1800s, the other being Richard Vipond (who had a foundry at Dock End). John Lowrie was also manufacturing metal items at the same period and had a brass foundry on St Anne's Staith.

As would be expected from a seaside port, graves of master mariners abound, but there are other trades waiting to be found on some of these stones – including sailors, a seamstress, a whitesmith, and a flax dresser, to name only a few. Somewhere, lost amongst the pathways beneath the south transept of the church, is the grave of a nine-year-old child who died from drowning, having met his end by falling off the end of Whitby pier sometime in the early 1800s. His companion at the time – who, it was thought, narrowly missed being washed off the pier by the same wave – later made a death-bed confession: he admitted that the incident had not been an accident at all, but instead that he

A rare example of a cast-iron grave marker. This one was produced at the Baxtergate foundry of engineer George Chapman in readiness for his own demise.

had lived a long and troubled life in the terrible, constant knowledge that it was he who had pushed his boyhood companion to his death in a fit of childhood anger.

The Parish Church

Memorials to those of a higher station, such as the lord of the manor and his family, together with other influential people in the town, will be found inside the old parish church where a number of graves and vaults are situated beneath ground level. In keeping with ancient tradition, their funerals would have been carried out at night under the light of flaming torches. We are told that King George was similarly buried by torchlight in London and that Sir

Peregrine Lascelles, a Whitby man who fought at the battle of Preston Pans, Scotland, in 1745, was buried in Whitby in the same manner three weeks after his death at York. A memorial stone to his memory can be seen in the church.

The inside of the building is frozen in time and its quaint box pews and hand-painted scripture boards are a delight not to be missed – especially during evening services, when the building is lit by candles. These box pews were once owned and rented in the same way as other property in Whitby. The strange, higgledy-piggledy layout instantly takes the visitor back to Victorian times, and there are dark, hidden corners where strange oddities are waiting to be discovered on each visit. Among these are a 'charity shelf' on which visitors could leave bread for the poor, a three-decker pulpit with old-fashioned ear trumpets for the hard of hearing, and an ancient child's coffin made of stone. On the rear wall, old photographs and press cuttings detail the more recent history of the church, whilst a collection of very old stone carvings belonging to the church's original structure reveal its more distant past. Look out also for the ancient 'Parish Chest', which can only be opened by three people at the same time, each carrying different keys, and the rescued medieval church fonts found

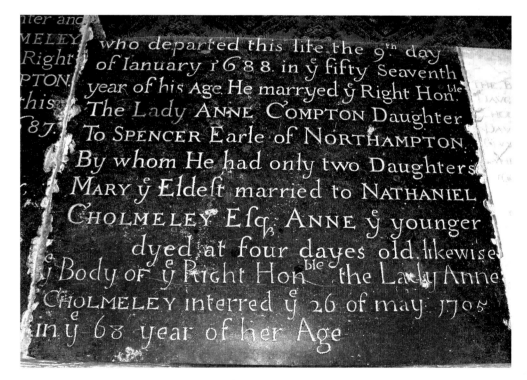

A gravestone set in the floor of the interior of St Mary's Church, close to the altar. It is one of a number that serve as memorials to the lives of the town's former aristocracy who were always buried inside the building.

The unusual higgledy-piggledy interior of St Mary's Church with its three-decker pulpit and balcony pew built right across the opening to the main altar area fascinates all who see it.

near Newbiggin Hall (where they had been used by a farmer as water troughs in one of his fields).

We are told in Charlton's *History of Whitby* that in former times there were a number of side chapels or smaller altars within the main church. According to Shaw Jeffrey in his *Whitby Lore and Legend*, these were possibly dedicated to St Catherine, the Holy Trinity, St Peter and the Altar of the Assumption, though another one may have been dedicated to the archangel Gabriel, as in the 1500s Mary Todd of York left twenty marks to build such an altar in the parish church.

It becomes obvious when examining the interior layout that it has been built and refurbished by local craftsmen who were more used to fitting out ships and boats than land-based constructions. The style is quite appropriate when we consider that the area of a church where the congregation sits is called the Nave (Latin for ship). As if to emphasise this, the main candelabra chandelier is hung from a small anchor, and indeed the whole structure of the church represents the lower decks of a ship, complete with wooden ceiling and small, high-set windows. These windows can give the interior a brooding, Gothic feel on dull, dark days, though the church can never be said to have a malevolent or eerie atmosphere (even in winter, when the building is devoid of its usual summer

Just some of the interesting exhibits on show within the church include old carved stones (top); the Parish Chest (centre left); a baby's coffin (centre right) made of stone; and an ancient carved chimera head (bottom).

The interior of the old parish church. The walls are covered in many interesting ancient wooden memorial boards and stone carvings, though perhaps none so Gothic as this one showing a flying skull.

crowds). Despite its long history (parts of it are older than the nearby abbey structure), there appear to be virtually no records of ghostly activity inside the church. Instead, the building evokes a timeless, calm and tranquil feeling which no doubt owes much to the strong community bonds that have permeated every nook and cranny of its fascinating and maze-like layout.

The only mention of ghosts found in connection with the building is a note regarding a vigil that took place annually on the eve of St Mark (24 April) near the old wooden porchway (now removed) that once stood over the central doorway to the right of the present entrance. It was believed that at midnight, shadowy figures would be seen passing through the wooden door into the graveyard, and that these silent, ghostly apparitions represented all those who were to die within the following year. In Victorian times, when the vigil had already become only a memory, the church authorities played down the story and banned residents of the town from entering the churchyard on that

An ancient hand-written board fixed to the wall still proclaims the Ten Commandments.

particular night. This, however, did not stop crowds gathering on the nearby Church Lane (alternatively known as the Donkey Road or Loaning) at midnight on St Mark's Eve so as to peer over the wall in the hope of spotting the ghostly figures for themselves.

Another weird custom which took place on the same evening was the sifting of hearth ashes around the fireplace in each house, the idea being that if any of the family were destined to die within the coming year their shoe print would mysteriously appear in the ash by the following morning. One wonders how seriously this portend of death was taken, and how often mischievous or ill-willed jokes were played on unsuspecting residents by pushing their shoes into the scattered ashes when everyone else was asleep.

One of the church's quaint curiosities is in the form of a neo-pagan circular temple that greets visitors as they enter through the porchway. This odd memorial to Whitby's lifeboat men was purchased by a previous clergyman, named Keane, who it is said bought it on a whim in Marylebone Road, London in 1853. It is interesting to note that whilst not identical, it is styled on similar lines to Marylebone All Soul's Church, which is not far as the crow flies from the round temple church associated with the Knights Templar, mentioned in Dan Brown's book *The Da Vinci Code*.

Another of the delights of the church interior is the often-missed area directly beneath the ancient church tower where the bell ringers gather. It is atmospherically lined with dark, aged, hand-painted boards recording, amongst other things, the campanology exploits of past years. Hiding away in the corner of this small space, though not generally accessible to visitors, is an original worn medieval spiral stone staircase that leads to the bell tower chamber. The claustrophobic climb, lit only by the occasional tiny window, is not for the faint-hearted, and looks and feels as though it belongs to the plot of some Victorian Gothic novel. The tiny, narrow sandstone steps are worn away and still have loose sand particles upon them, serving as a reminder of the erosion caused by scores of human feet over hundreds of years. To climb these steps is to experience an eerie sense of travelling into the past as they curl around in a dizzy, tight spiral, allowing little space for the shoulders, let alone elbow room. It is not unknown for those who have attempted the claustrophobic climb to turn back, being unable to cope with the very confined space, and it must be said that almost everyone experiences a profound feeling of relief when the summit is reached and one finally emerges into the part of the tower where the old church bells hang. To be in this chamber on a dull, windy day is an eerie experience in itself. The tower appears to move with each howling gust of wind and it is hard to imagine that this apparently frail structure has survived the full blast of North Sea gales for hundreds of years.

A small doorway leading from the bell chamber leads onto the tower roof where spectacular views of the surrounding area, including the sea and Whitby Abbey, come into sight. Though the abbey once had a fine bell tower of its own, it fell to the ground shortly after a local chimney sweep climbed it for a bet to retrieve its copper weather vane in 1830. In its time it was said to have a loud peal of bells that could be heard by pilgrims and travellers as far away as Thornton le Dale and Hackness. At the time of the dissolution of the monasteries, the bells were removed and the noise which for centuries had sounded over land and sea was replaced by an eerie silence. Their removal is said to have prompted genuine anger amongst the residents of the town and surrounding area. Even further outrage was expressed when they were loaded on a ship in Whitby Harbour ready for transportation to London. Crowds of local people are said to have gathered at the pier end as the ship sailed out, many of them chanting primitive ancient curses against those that had stolen their heritage. Local legend says that the curses were effective, and immediately the ship had left the port a storm blew up out of nowhere: shortly afterwards the ship, its crew and its cargo sank to the bottom of the sea near Whitby Rock where, according to legend, they lie to this day.

There were, until recently, residents who insisted that on stormy nights, a person standing on the pier end could still hear the stolen bells ringing below the waves. Others, however, insist that the sound that was heard was the old bell buoy which was anchored a mile off Whitby to alert ships of the treacherous underwater rocks. Its weird, muted bell was indeed a strange sound as it drifted through the fog. In recent times, a modern electronic marine device replaced it. Like the sound of the Hawsker 'Bawling Bull' fog horn that once eerily floated across the cliffs towards the town, the haunting sound of the bell buoy has disappeared – and with its demise another Whitby legend has been confined to the history books forever.

In 1773, when this engraving was produced, the tower and much more of the main structure were still in place. The tower collapsed in 1830.

Chanted verses of the kind uttered at the stealing of the abbey bells were in the past commonly used under many circumstances, including one used by children of fishermen and seamen who were overdue in returning home from the sea. It was a widespread practice in these circumstances for groups of children to be sent to the cliff top where they would chant: 'Suther wind suther, suther wind suther. And blow me father home to me mother'. Very few of these old magical chants remain, though schoolchildren in playgrounds even today, at the first sign of snowflakes, can be heard trying to bring on a snowstorm by jointly chanting: 'Ally Ally Aster, Snow Snow Faster' . Others try to influence the unwanted presence of rain with: 'Rain, Rain, go away, come again another day.'

To many visitors the parish church appears to be little more than a quaint museum piece, but this could not be further from the truth. St Mary's continues to serve the local community as a place of worship and for the celebration of christenings and weddings. Even though burials in the old churchyard are now closed, funeral services occasionally take place here. Most funeral parties now arrive by motor hearse, though in older times local residents did not consider themselves 'properly churched' unless they had climbed (or been carried up) the 199 steps to be christened, married or buried.

It was common in earlier times for coffins to be 'hand-carried' from the bottom of the steps to the top with bearers supporting the coffin with white linen towels or sheets. Only males would carry a dead man, whilst women carried the coffins of a female. Similarly, youths would act as pall bearers when the deceased was himself or herself a young adult, and babies would be carried under the arm of a female. Should a woman die in childbirth, her coffin would be covered with a white sheet. On these occasions songs would be sung by a small group walking in front of the funeral cortege – unless the person being buried was a virgin, in which case two virgins dressed in white would take their place carrying a hoop bedecked with flowers and a white glove in the centre. The glove would have the initials of the deceased person embroidered upon it. Following the funeral, the hoops would be hung in the rafters of the church.

Those who have ascended these steps will have been thankful for the wide steps and seats placed at various stages on the steep incline. Few realise that these are in fact 'coffin stops' and both the benches and wide steps were placed there not for the benefit of visitors but 'for the easement of bearers': in other words, to give those in the funeral procession a chance to catch their breath on the way up and a place to rest the coffin whilst they did so.

From the upper gallery of the church's old windows, visitors can look down on the harbour entrance and Tate Hill beach where the *Dmitri* came aground in 1885. These same windows are the ones described in chapter eight of *Dracula*:

I was quite a little startled myself, for it seemed for an instant as if the stranger had great eyes like burning flames, but a second look dispelled the illusion. The red sunlight was shining on the windows of St Mary's Church behind our seat, and as the

Left: A couple of Goths climb the 199 steps towards one of the benches (bottom left) which originally served the purpose of coffin rests for funeral bearers. **Right:** A view of Whitby from the upper galleries of the parish church. In the mid-foreground is Tate Hill Beach where Dracula's ship was washed ashore in the novel.

sun dipped there was just sufficient change in the refraction and reflection to make it appear as if the light moved.

The red sunlight effect mentioned in this passage is real and must have been observed by Stoker during his stay in the town. On a summer's evening as the sun begins to slowly set in the sea (itself a phenomenon that occurs in only two places on Britain's coastline), the windows of the parish church begin to glow blood-red, giving the scene an eerie appearance when observed from the West Cliff.

CHAPTER THREE

Tonsures and Dirty Habits

Saints and Sinners at Whitby Abbey

The vow of chastity led to problems with the Medieval nuns... Nuns became pregnant... Moral standards declined and Nuns... also enjoyed forbidden luxuries such as dancing, fine foods, and lapdogs.

(http://www.middle-ages.org.uk)

It should be remembered that the saintly abbess Hilda never lived in the structure we call Whitby Abbey, because these ruins are all that remains of a later church used by the male-orientated Benedictine Order. Hilda's original abbey may have been merely a small wooden structure surrounded by circular dwellings where both male and female adherents to the faith, including family groups, lived together under her rule. There has been speculation that the parish church, itself older in parts than the abbey, could have been the site of St Hilda's church, but there is no hard evidence to prove this. Most of what we know about St Hilda – or Hild, as she was called – is derived from the writings of the Venerable Bede, a northern monk whose tomb can still be seen in Durham Cathedral.

The only ancient picture of St Hilda that exists appears on one side of the old abbey bulla seal. Both sides are reproduced here, together with a modern image of the saint.

Bede tells us that she was the daughter of Hereric, the nephew of King Edwin of Northumbria, and that her first post as abbess was at Hartlepool, where she ruled another double monastery consisting of monks and nuns before moving on to Whitby. Historians disagree as to whether Whitby was called by its ancient name of Streonshalch (various spellings) at that time, or whether it was a name that came about at a later date. Some have continued to put forward the old theory that the name meant 'Streon's settlement', though often without any explanation or evidence to back up the claim. The word 'hale' or 'hall', according to John Richardson in his classic *Local Historian's Encyclopaedia*, does in fact mean 'a small corner of land', and as such would fit in with the 'Streon's settlement' theory exactly, but only if a person such as Streon was proved to exist. In fact, Streon, or, more correctly, Eadric Streona, did exist, though it was in the far later Viking period. More interestingly, he played a prominent part in the early history of Viking England – as did the town of Whitby, which still retains many Viking words in its local dialect. Streona was evidently a ruthless and self-seeking double-dealer who just happened to be the son-in-law of King Ethelred. It is recorded that he later became the Earl of Mercia, having murdered many of the supporters of the old Mercian ruling families. A political commentator of the time described the situation after 1017:

For Swein's son Canute had recruited the flower of Viking Europe, and Ethelred's son, Edmund Ironside could not remake England. In four great battles he revived some of the old Wessex loyalty, but Thorkill, offended by Ethelred's double dealing, joined Canute, and the double traitor Eadric Streona likewise – who was pardoned, but only to ruin Edmund again by deserting him in the last battle of Ashingdon in 1016. The Earl of Northumbria, and the Danelaw, outraged and betrayed by Streona, would not pit themselves against the invader alone...

History goes on to tell us that Canute became 'King of all England' in 1016-17, and if by this time the turncoat Eadric Streona was still on the side of Canute, it is possible he could have been awarded a 'small corner of land' (a hale) for his efforts. If so, could Streona's hale or Streonschalh have been established here at Whitby as it was at Strensall near York? As the Strensall parish's website explains, 'Strensall is referred to in the Doomsday book as Streonaeshalch, after Streona – a name, and halch – a corner of land. The land was owned by the Church and in particular the Bishops at York'.

Whatever the truth, many historians believe that St Hilda began administering Streonshalch abbey under that name at an earlier time when ancient Paganism was merging with Christianity, causing many disagreements amongst followers of both religious lifestyles. This culminated in the Synod of Whitby in AD 664 when the calculating of religious festivals, including Easter, using astronomical criteria was set for all time by the church leaders in the precincts of Hilda's abbey.

Burials

The synod of AD 664 secured a high position in the early Christian church for both Hilda and her abbey, so much so that many members of royalty and the Church made regular visits to Whitby, including King Oswy (Oswiu) of Northumbria (who was buried here). Also interred at Whitby Abbey was the torso of King (Saint) Edwin of Deira. St Edwin was slain in battle on 12 October AD 633, and though his body was laid to rest at Whitby, his head was conveyed to St Peter's Church at York in recognition of his act of founding the church there.

William de Percy, known as the First Baron Percy, was also buried in the grounds of the old abbey. He was a rich Yorkshire landholder who was involved in the rebuilding of York Castle after it was sacked by the Vikings in 1070. Two years later he was fighting for William the Conqueror in Scotland. He built Topcliffe Castle, but more importantly refounded Whitby Abbey in 1086. William joined the First Crusade as a knight but died in battle. Though he was buried at Mount Joy, Jerusalem, he left instructions with another knight, Sir Ralph Eversly, that his heart should be brought back to Whitby. Sir Ralph personally attended to William de Percy's request and saw that his heart was buried in the grounds of Whitby Abbey. William de Percy left behind a number of sons, and one of these, also named William, became the second abbot at Whitby.

Regardless of these significant burials, it has become clear that not only important people were buried in the abbey grounds. In recent years a medieval graveyard was excavated to the south of the abbey ruins, revealing over a hundred ancient graves. These relatively shallow graves may have provided the last resting place of monks or local citizens of the town, or perhaps both. They were found in a now grassy area that strangely once had a reputation as a haunted field, according to those staying at Abbey House. In the 1930s a number of guests apparently reported having observed strange misty figures moving across the area on dark, foggy nights. The graves discovered during the excavations appear to have been laid in tight regular rows, and though evidence of a few coffin burials was found, on the whole they seem to show that most of the bodies were buried in shrouds alone. Few objects were discovered other than a sceatta coin, dating from around AD 700, shroud pins and a glass gaming piece. Several of the burials may in fact be Roman, but experts have failed to agree on exactly from what date in the abbey's history the cemetery belongs.

The dig in 1999 also revealed some rather odd burials, including a number of cases where the bodies were buried face down with their hands tied behind their backs and two bodies that were decapitated with their heads being buried at their feet and with their jaws facing away from their bodies. In some cases the bodies may also have been tied at the knees. On the whole, the bodies were buried in an East-West direction, indicating Christian burials.

The Ghost of St Hilda

Most experts believe that St Hilda was originally buried in the grounds of her own abbey at Whitby following a long seven-year illness described as a 'fever'. Her bones are said to later have been 'translated' to Glastonbury under the orders of King Edmund (though others argue that the story is merely a myth and that she was eventually laid to rest at Gloucester). In reality, in line with religious practices at that time, it is likely that her 'holy' bones may have been distributed throughout the country, finding their way to reliquaries in various churches throughout the land. Her ghost is still said to haunt the abbey and Charlton, in his *History of Whitby* in 1779 gave precise instructions for seeing the ghost:

> ...she still renders herself visible on some occasions in the Abbey... At a particular time of the year (namely in the summer months) at ten or eleven in the forenoon, the sunbeams fall in the inside of the northern part of the choir, and 'tis then that the spectators who stand on the west side of Whitby Churchyard, so as just to see the north side of the Abbey past the north end of Whitby Church, imagine they perceive, in one of the highest windows there, the resemblance of a woman dressed in a shroud... The very form of Hilda fair, hovering upon the sunny air.

Carnal Pleasures

The ghostly image that many have claimed to have seen at the window within the ruins at night, when the moon is in the right position, may have nothing whatsoever to do with St Hilda at all. Some believe it is instead the ghost of a young nun who was reputedly bricked up in the abbey walls many centuries ago. Whether this actually occurred here or not is open to question, but the practice has been noted in other areas, where in ancient times nuns would be temporarily bricked up in a small crevice for varying periods as a penance. Their only sustenance was some pieces of bread and water to last them through their ordeal. At Coldingham Priory, for example, the punishment was common for nuns who had broken their vows of chastity. The skeleton of a female was discovered there in Victorian times sitting in a crouched position in a small bricked-up niche. The question is, was she simply forgotten, did she die before they released her, or were more sinister motives afoot?

How these nuns came to break their vows of chastity is no great mystery when we look at old monastic records. At the nunnery at North Berwick, for instance, a former prioress expressed her concerns regarding the regular practice of certain nuns who would climb over the walls at night like naughty boarding-school pupils in order to make visits to the young men in a nearby village. Such incidents were not uncommon, and despite our modern conceptions, it appears that the nuns of that time lived far from saintly lives. At Basedale Priory near Whitby in May 1307, Archbishop Corbridge ordered the seizing of the goods belonging to the nuns, ordering them to be transferred to Roger de Kelleshay, the rector of Crathorne. The reason given for this mass confiscation was the excesses and perpetual misdeeds of the prioress, Joan de Percy and her nuns. The nuns did not take the matter lying down though – so to speak – and Joan de Percy, together with a number of her nuns, walked out in protest, leading to the archbishop demanding they should not go beyond the precincts of the monastery but should 'serve God in the cloister under the yoke of obedience' instead.

In 1308 another Yorkshire nun named Agnes de Thormondby was described as being in a 'miserable state' having on three occasions succumbed to deception and the commitment of *carnis decepta blandiciis* (carnal enticement). Whether this involved actual pregnancy is not stated, but some monasteries are said to have had a reputation for killing the illegitimate children of nuns at birth and depositing them in a special 'birth pit' reserved for the purpose.

Unruly Monks

Monks were also known for breaking or bending the rules, and the ones at Whitby Abbey were no exception. On the contrary, far from living a pious life, there is evidence that theft, corruption and ill-feeling were a constant monastic theme. Holt in his *Whitby Past & Present*, tells us that when the monks left the precincts of Whitby Abbey they were obliged to travel in twos, presumably to keep each other out of mischief. At night they all slept in the same dormitory and slept in their day clothes 'but never two in a bed'. We also know that, 'Every monk had two coats, two cowls, a table book, a knife, a needle, and a handkerchief; the furniture of his bed was a mat, a blanket, a rug and a pillow'.

A traditional view of monks at work in a scriptorium. Old records show that monastic life was not always as idealistic as this.

Despite the reputation of monks for peace and harmony, there are at least two stories which show that, when necessary, they were not above having a good punch-up. One happened during the celebrations at the feast of St Hilda when Whitby fishermen processed through the town carrying burning tar barrels. Having had a drop too many, a number of drunken seafarers decided they would climb the steps to the abbey in order to have a bit of fun at the expense of the monks. Whether this was a regular occurrence or whether the monks had been forewarned is not clear, but the fishermen got more than they bargained for: waiting in hiding at the top of the church steps were a bunch of young monks who wasted no time in giving the fishermen a good thrashing before chasing them back down the steps into the town.

The website www.british-history.ac.uk gives an account of another similar incident:

On the eves of Midsummer, St Peter and St Thomas, a bonfire was made in Whitby and neighbouring towns, and the mariners and fishermen went in procession with half a burning tar barrel borne before them on a staff, carrying what weapons they pleased...

but on the last St Peter's Eve the abbot's servants [the monks]... had fallen on them and shamefully beaten them. The abbot pretended ignorance and offered to give them ale on St Thomas's Eve, but as they climbed the narrow approach to the abbey they were again set upon, driven into the town and badly hurt.

Old records such as this give us a fascinating insight into the monastic period and makes us reassess our vision of what life in the cloisters was like at that time. In October 1366, for instance, Utred, the senior scholar of the Benedictine Order in York, received reports of constant unruly behaviour by the monks at Whitby Abbey and ordered his officers to conduct an official inquiry. No fewer than fifty-six charges were brought against Matthew Dawney (also known as D'Alney), the prior, who was a bitter opponent of the abbot at that time. Nine charges were also made against Thomas of Haukesgard [Hawsker] who was a former abbot and another two against a monk named Robert of Boynton.

The courts were told that Matthew Dawney, together with other monks, including Robert of Boynton, John of Rychemond (Richmond), Johannes of Allerton, John of Levyngton (Levington), John of Marton, William of Ormesby, and William of Darum (Durham) had collaborated with Thomas of Haukesgard to be disobedient to the abbot. These monks, it was alleged, had caused dilapidation of the abbey property to the extent that the abbey buildings were described as 'destroyed and fallen down' so that many of the monks had nowhere sheltered to live in. The inference was that a rebellious group of the monks had stolen and/or misused the property for their own ends. Furthermore, the monk Robert of Boynton was described as being 'beyond correction' in that he was a 'seeker of personal pleasure'. The charge was that he had had regular sex with a Rosedale nun, Katherine Megeir. The monk supposedly kept the nun as his personal mistress and was sending her goods which belonged to the abbey. Among these items were five silver spoons belonging to the abbey guest house. He was also charged with missing abbey services in order to visit the 'vill of Whitby' for pleasurable purposes (despite previous warnings not only from the abbot but also directly from the Archbishop of York).

The Calendar Rolls (Vol. X1V, page sixty-one) show that a royal inquiry was instituted into this unacceptable state of disarray. Witnesses were sought not only from within the abbey community but from Whitby residents also. They were ordered to give evidence under oath concerning the alleged corruption, misappropriation of goods and lack of maintenance which they claimed had led to the normal monastic functions of prayer and almsgiving falling into misuse.

A few years later, in April 1371, the arrest and punishment of Thomas of Hawks Garth (Hawsker) was ordered: however, this did not stop further unrest and ill-feeling towards the abbot, and the troubles continued unabated. The following month Alexander of Lith (Lythe), the abbey's steward, found himself accused of 'scheming with others to destroy the abbot's office' and of misappropriating the abbey's goods to the extent that the monks could not carry out their normal duties. It was feared by the authorities that the innocent monks had just about had enough of the constant bickering and that they were at the point of leaving the abbey altogether. Lith was further accused of having stolen the abbey seal and is said to have dissipated the abbot's goods as well as the abbey's. There was also the mysterious matter of a monk having in his possession 300 counterfeit florins which he claimed were not his own but which belonged to the abbot, causing him (the abbot) to be detained in York Castle prison. The question remains as to who the counterfeit coins actually belonged to – and more to the point, where were they manufactured? Could it possibly be that they were made in the abbey by the band of medieval forgers passing themselves off as monks, and that Whitby Abbey was the headquarters of some sort of counterfeit florin-making factory?

CHAPTER FOUR

Ghosts, Wraiths and Spectres

A Guide to Haunted Whitby

Apparitions, both before and after death, are of course not infrequent in Whitby. Many a valuable house has stood untenanted for years on the suspicion of being haunted, the last residents having experienced considerable alarm and anxiety; the bed curtains having been undrawn, the bed clothes torn off, the window shutters unloosed, the china broken, the furniture demolished, and numerous other supernatural occurrences are stated to have taken place.

(Shaw Jeffrey – local author)

It would be very surprising indeed if a town with a history as old as Whitby's did not have a reputation for ghostly activity. Today there are still many old buildings that have a reputation for having at least one residential ghost. Most of them, luckily enough, are said to be of the friendly kind. Shaw Jeffrey, in his *Whitby Lore and Legend*, quotes an article from the *Whitby Repository* of 1828 showing that the town had a reputation regarding hauntings of various kinds even at that time:

Strange traditions exist of certain yards, lanes and alleys; of some terrible homicide there committed; of departed spirits that have walked for several nights successively, deprived

This eighteenth-century woodcut shows what superstitious people of the time believed ghosts, spirits and hobgoblins looked like.

of their rest, desirous of being addressed by someone, but none daring; of hearses and mourning coaches that have been seen to drive past at midnight, the horses without heads or with white sheets on their backs; and numerous other equally credible reports; the whole of which most of the inhabitants fearfully believe.

Wraiths and Waffs

Wraiths and waffs are ghostly apparitions in the form of a living person that appear prior to their death. Two examples are recorded in 1879 by William Henderson, in his book *Folklore of the Northern Counties*. The first case involved a respectable eighty-two-year-old man who recalled a boyhood incident in his home village of Danby, near Whitby. Passing a house, the man recalled seeing his uncle through the window of the sitting room, despite the fact that for many years the man was known to have been totally 'bedfast'. Entering the room, the boy was surprised to find it in complete darkness and the seat he had seen his uncle sitting in completely empty. When he told his mother of the incident she immediately suspected that the boy had seen a wraith. Sure enough, his uncle's death took place shortly afterwards. In another case recorded by the same author, a Whitby tradesman suffering from kidney stones was ordered by his doctor to go to York hospital for an operation. He surprised his medic and his family by telling them that the operation was doomed to failure as he had already seen his own waff. The man was nevertheless persuaded to attend York Hospital and was successfully operated upon. Strangely, as he had predicted, despite the medical success of the operation he died soon afterwards.

Henderson, who told the story, believed that had the man been mentally prepared he could have prevented his demise: as all old Yorkshire folk know, when seeing one's own waff the prospect of death is not inevitable. The way to deal with a waff, he explained, was to confront it and to send it packing:

> Had he spoken to it, all would have been well. Thus a native of Guisborough, on going into a shop at Whitby, saw his own 'waff,' and boldly addressed it thus: 'What's thou doin' here? What's thou doin' here? Thou's after no good, I'll go bail! Get thy ways yom wi' thee. Get thy ways yom!' The result of his thus taking the initiative was perfectly satisfactory.

Abbey Precincts

A number of ghostly experiences have occurred from time to time in and around the abbey grounds. Some of these sightings have been experienced by travellers staying at the old Youth Hostel building. The YHA has recently moved location, but for many years had its home at the left-hand side of the long, low building that stands to the right of the parish church, bordering Almshouse Close (known locally as Jacky Fields, i.e. Jackass Fields). The building has been called the 'abbey stables', but probably was used both as combined stables and visitors' quarters and in effect served as an almshouse. Various stories have emerged of ghostly figures moving through the dormitories at night with dark, hooded figures apparently passing through the walls or being seen walking from room to room.

Residents of Caedmon House, which is situated at the southernmost end of the same block of buildings, have also described an 'atmosphere' in its upper bedrooms with the sound of monks being heard chanting by both day and night. A crucifix was found by a former resident hidden in a small cavity in one of the bedroom's ancient beams, indicating that others before them had also experienced strange happenings. Another odd occurrence reported as taking place at Caedmon House was the intermittent pleasant smell of cooked food wafting through the building even though no cooking was taking place. This latter ghostly occurrence may however have a more earthly explanation: it has been speculated that the whole building block may have an ancient hidden under-croft space stretching along its full length. If this is so, then the cooking smells emanating from the interior of Caedmon House may actually have had their origins in the modern kitchens of the Youth Hostel at the other end of the same block.

Caedmon House is believed to be part of the old abbey almshouse and stables' structure. This picture shows the windows of the upper story where ghostly activity has been reported.

Bagdale Hall

As Whitby's oldest inhabited dwelling, Bagdale Hall has long held a reputation for being the town's most haunted building. The hall's long and chequered history has no doubt contributed to this situation, for in its time it has been home to toffs and tramps, rich men and bankrupts and at least one political rebel, Browne Bushel, a Royalist officer who was beheaded in London for treason in 1651. His headless ghost is said to have been spotted on a number of occasions haunting the upper floors of the building on the anniversary of his execution.

Bagdale Hall was originally constructed as a manor house in the early 1500s by James Conyers, a sergeant at arms to King Henry VIII and bailiff to the Abbot of Whitby Abbey. At that time, the hall was an isolated building described as being situated on the outskirts of the town and surrounded by fields. A small wooden bridge once crossed 'Bagdale Beck', a small tidal stream which at one time ran along the bottom of the hall's garden wall but which is now covered over by the present roadway. Residents of the building were known to catch fish from

Bagdale Hall as it appears today. A small tidal river (known locally as a beck) once ran through its front garden and along what is now Bagdale. Fish were frequently caught from the hall's windows.

its bedroom windows. In 1631, Isaac Newton of Ruswarp bought the property for £1,800, by which time it already had a reputation for 'strange goings on'.

It was known as Bagdale 'Old' Hall, even in 1734 when it was surrounded by lands known as Bagdale Estate. These grounds included gardens, a bleaching garth, the 'Great Pasture', a cottage and other open fields stretching from 'Backdale Beck' to Bog Hall, together with lands covering both sides of what is now Spring Hill as far as the present railway station. The occupants of the hall at that time also owned the Horse Mill in Baxtergate, close to what is now known as Boots Corner. This Horse Mill was originally a building using horses (possibly to drive a mechanism to open and close the bridge as well as for grinding its owner's grain). It was still in existence in 1817 and described as being in Horse Mill Ghaut, a ghaut being a local name for a passage leading to a slipway for accessing the harbour. The building was at that time used for grinding malt. In the same ghaut was a 'house' belonging to Christopher Richardson which was used as wine cellars. The building continued to serve this purpose until the time of its last owners, Falkingbridge & Son. At that time it was on maps as the former 'St Ninian's Chapel'.

In 1769, local shipowner John Walker purchased Bagdale Hall but is said to never have been happy with it, attributing its 'malevolent spirits' to a string of financial failures which resulted in him selling the building in 1826 to his son-in-law, Wakefield Simpson. Simpson also disliked living there and left after an occupancy of only two years.

An interesting description of the once open area known as Victoria Square, situated between Bagdale Hall and the Roman Catholic church, was given by Robert B. Holt, F.R.S.L. He recalled Bagdale Beck as it was in his younger days, when he lived in a building on the site of what is now the George Hotel and Rosy O'Grady's pub:

> In 1830 we were living in the house in Baxtergate, now known as the Station Hotel. At that time the lower part of Bagdale Beck was uncovered, and from a gallery which connected the upper floors of a couple of out-house that overlooked the beck; we occasionally caught fish in it at high water. Victoria square was then an enclosed paddock, and at the east end there were stepping stones on which you crossed the beck at low tide. Just before it reached the harbour some warehouses abutted on the beck. Under one end of them was a darkish passage through which you passed to the ship-yards, to be welcomed by a colony of rooks who tenanted some tall elms which flourished at the further end of it, and to be confronted by the Stocks which there awaited all evil-doers.

By the late 1800s the ancient hall was said to be deteriorating rapidly, to such an extent that the upper floors became a doss house for visiting tramps who tore up the floorboards and burnt the decorative Elizabethan panelling in order to keep warm during the winter months. A number of them, it is said, died there, one of them having been mortally injured when the original rotten wooden stairs, which had also been plundered for firewood, collapsed completely.

Eventually, the building was shut up. Repairs were eventually made to its inner structures in 1883 by its new owner, Henry Power, a noted opthalmic surgeon who decorated the original fireplace and other areas with spectacular wooden embellishments and blue delft tiles. During the period in which it was closed up completely, local people are said to have avoided the building at night: strange swirling ghostly-coloured lights could allegedly be seen glinting through the broken windows, a phenomenon that also occurred in another building which stood diagonally opposite at the end of Baxtergate.

In 1914, Mr and Mrs Percy Shaw Jeffrey bought Bagdale Hall. Shaw Jeffrey had a keen interest in the occult and was said to have lived in total harmony with the many spirits that occupied the building. Visitors reported bumps in the night, doors that would mysteriously open on their own and lights that would turn on and off; on one occasion a cleaner reported that a feather duster was dragged

This old advert for Falkingbridges wine and spirits merchants from the 1800s shows their warehouse building (which is believed to have been the original St Ninian's chapel).

from her hand by some invisible force and began floating around the room for quite some time. After the death of Percy Shaw Jeffrey, the building was left to Whitby Literary and Philosophical Society and reputedly the former owner's ashes were buried in a recess in the wall facing Bagdale. In later years they were removed and now lie in a niche in the wall of the interior of the parish church.

During the interim period, just before it was sold to a private buyer, a group of local town politicians discussed the building's reputation for being haunted, fearing its resident ghosts might prevent anyone from wanting to purchase it. One particularly sceptical Whitby councillor disagreed, saying that its reputation was all in the mind. Following a heated disagreement he agreed to spend a night alone in the haunted building for a bet. Those who remember the incident said that no tricks were played upon him during his attempted sleep-in but that his scepticism gave way to firm belief in the supernatural within only

After the death of Percy Shaw Jeffrey, his ashes are said to have been placed in a niche in the northern wall of Bagdale Hall. Today they rest in the parish church together with those of his wife.

Left: High up on the peak of the roof of Bagdale Hall is a pelican. It replaced an earlier one depicted in the process of plucking its own feathers to feed its young, a mystical symbol of self-sacrifice. **Right:** The old carving showing George and the Dragon undoubtedly came to Whitby from Venice, though experts disagree as to whether it is the original tablet discussed by Ruskin in his work *The Stones of Venice* or simply a well-designed copy.

The Shaw Jeffrey's were avid collectors of the unusual, but where did these religious sculptures that lay at the side of the old hall come from?

a few hours. Shortly after midnight, he fled the building saying that he could stand it no longer after the empty building had 'unexplainably come alive'. The interior was at that time described as immensely interesting and atmospheric. It was decorated with ancient lettered inscriptions, old shop and inn signs, date plaques, monograms, coats of arms, lead fire insurance plaques, symbolic carvings and statues contained within secret niches.

The exterior also holds some mysteries and secrets of its own. Among these is the statue of a pelican on the gable end of the roof: this pelican replaced an even older figure showing a pelican plucking out its feathers whilst feeding its young with its own blood, a classic mystical symbol of self sacrifice. Also at the rear of the building is a now worn stone tablet showing another kind of sacrifice, namely that of the killing of a dragon by St George. In March 1993, this carved tablet was discussed in papers drawn up on behalf of a firm of solicitors. Their aim was to decide what parts of the building were considered fixtures and fittings pending its sale. The sculptured George and the dragon plaque is alleged to date from the sixteenth or seventeenth century and to have come directly from Venice, having been mentioned in Ruskin's work, the *Stones of Venice*. The report seems to cast doubt on the fact that this is the self-same original piece, and reminds the reader that, 'It should be borne in mind that Italian artists have been selling antiques to tourists for a long time and have almost as good a reputation for 'reproductions' as the Chinese'. According to Vassari, Michelangelo's first assay at sculpture was in the production of imitation antiques for resale to sixteenth-century tourists. Despite this query with regards to its authenticity, the sculpture was considered quite valuable, with a replacement value in modern times of around £20,000.

Along the side of the building are some interesting sculptures, possibly rescued from an old church, whose origins are unknown.

Baxtergate

The whole area around the western end of Baxtergate seems to have an eerie reputation. Strange things regularly occurred in a building that once extended into the centre of Brunswick Street. Like Bagdale Hall, it was also reputably haunted by unearthly swirling lights, and curious townsfolk would gather on the

Two truncated windows are all that remains of a building said to have been demolished because its hauntings attracted too much attention.

hillside at night – on the spot where the Catholic church now stands – to watch the goings on. If legend is to be believed, the local authorities became so fed up with the stories circulating around the town that they ordered the building be demolished. All that remains of the house today are the truncated stone window frames; they can still be seen on the Baxtergate side of the present end building of the street.

Strangely, a similar story of ghostly figures and coloured lights being watched from exactly the same bank led to the demolition of an even older building on the same site at an earlier period. The residential building owned by the Holt family was the home of a well-known local surgeon, Dr Ripley. The family who lived there became so disturbed – not by the ghosts, but by the crowds of regular onlookers – that they moved into Brunswick House, Skate Lane (now Brunswick Street). The haunted house stood empty for a number of years before being demolished, and its building materials were recycled to construct the present buildings that run from the George Hotel to the end of Baxtergate.

The Old Smuggler Café

The haunted old Smuggler Café, which is situated towards the centre of Baxtergate, has a long history as a tavern and actually does stand over a smuggler's tunnel which ran from the Old Cutty Sark Inn (now the Station Inn) on New Quay Road. The tunnel, which was once considered only a myth, was

The haunted Old Smuggler Café was once a tavern known as the Ship Launch Inn. It was in existence prior to 1740 when beer cost one penny for two quarts. The cheapness of its ale was no doubt due to the smuggling activities of its landlord, as a tunnel once connected its cellar with other buildings in the town.

discovered in recent years and parts of it have been found in the cellars of the Station Inn and in buildings in Loggerhead Yard. During demolition of buildings in Baxtergate prior to the construction of the present Boots Chemist's shop, a continuation of the tunnel was found running along the back of the earth bank leading towards the bridge. This probably connected with yet another tunnel which is reputed to have emerged under the font of the old chapel at the bottom of Flowergate. It may well have also connected with a known concealed smugglers' cellar in the former Talbot Hotel (now Talbot House) at the harbour end of Baxtergate.

The Old Smuggler Café is well known for the black figure attached to its frontage. Though it has been called the 'black Devil' by some of the Goth visitors, it is actually a small ship's figurehead or loggerhead, and gives its name to Loggerhead Yard in which the café's entrance is found. The figure was allegedly taken from a captured French smuggling ship brought into the harbour by the old 'Preventative Men' or customs officers. The inside of this café is quite atmospheric, with low ceilings that make the building feel as if time has stood still in it for hundreds of years. It is not surprising that workers over the years have claimed to have experienced the presence of at least one resident ghost. The word 'presence' is used advisably, because rather than exhibiting a physical form this particular spirit is known to push people gently by the arm, or shoulder, especially late at night or at the close of business. Perhaps this unassuming ghost is simply telling staff that they have worked enough and it is time to go home.

Whitby's Old Bridge

An early bridge over the Esk, now demolished, was said to have been haunted by a ghost from the animal kingdom in the form of a spectral horse. The horse is said to have always made its appearance on dark, tempestuous nights. No explanation was ever given for the haunting, but two incidents which occurred in the 1800s may cast some light on the legend. It is known that during that period a funeral coach driven by a man named Brown was returning across the bridge during stormy conditions, having just buried a well-known local character, John Falkingbridge. The hearse and its unfortunate horses were blown off the bridge by a strong gust of wind, drowning one of the two horses in the process.

A similar drowning of a horse was recorded here around the same time. On this occasion it broke away from its owner and jumped over the barrier fence whilst the bridge was closed to road traffic. Falling into the water, the unfortunate horse was dragged down by the carriage it was pulling, and, to the distress of both its owner and the crowd waiting to cross the bridge, it could not be recovered before it was claimed by its watery grave.

Unlike the present bridge, this earlier version swivelled. A barrier at the end didn't stop one particular horse from jumping over into the harbour and drowning. Its ghost may well have been one of the two spectral horses that haunted this area in the past.

White Horse and Griffin

This old tavern in Church Street has a number of supposed ghosts, many of which appear to be modern inventions. The building, however, is very ancient, and prior to its use as a restaurant it was used for the storage of various items, including fishermen's pots and nets. Many of those who used the building at that time reported a malevolent atmosphere, though no actual sightings of ghosts were ever recorded. It is said that despite a £50 reward to anyone who was prepared to stay in the dilapidated building overnight, no one was able to do so, including a group of professional ghost hunters who attempted to seek out the spirit(s) using scientific electrical equipment. Today, the ancient coaching inn, which once boasted Captain Cook and Charles Dickens as former customers, is a successful business once more. With its refurbishment, the malevolent spirit(s) appear to have gone forever, and guests can once more dine or sleep comfortably in their beds in peace - unless of course you know different!

The Turk's Head

The Turk's Head at 73 Church Street was fully or partly demolished in 1946 and had the reputation of being Whitby's most haunted public house. It was situated directly opposite the end of Grape Lane and was described as a fine, brick-built building with stone quoins. The same structure had once been the substantial townhouse of the Yeoman family but later had been divided up, with Porteus's shoe shop occupying the ground-floor level of the building. The whole structure is said to have had an 'evil' feel to it (even when it was a local drinking house and its dingy rooms were only frequented by the less desirable characters in the town). Dark tales circulated the town about its landlord, who was accused of being in league with the Devil. Rumours later circulated that the landlord had left the area without notice, seemingly vanishing without trace and leaving all his possessions in the rundown pub. Because a bar wench had gone missing at the same time, locals assumed that they had run off together. However, many years later, during alterations to the rear of the building, a long wooden box was supposedly discovered sealed up in a wall. Its discoverers were shocked to find that it contained the skeleton of a young female. Residents could only draw the conclusion that the skeleton was that of the barmaid who disappeared and

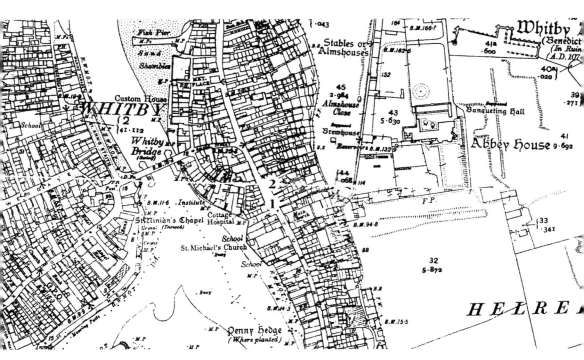

Part of Whitby as it was in 1929. The positions marked in the centre show Cockpit Yard [1] and the Turks Head [2], both of which were associated with hauntings.

that her body had lain undetected within the walls of the haunted building ever since she and the landlord had disappeared from the scene.

Cockpit Yard

An early ship's dry dock was discovered in recent years almost opposite the site of the Turk's Head during excavation work for the new sewer system. It existence had been previously unknown; it was filled in during the 1700s in order for buildings to be erected upon the site. Amongst these buildings in the Tattie Market area (Tattie rhymes with Matey) was the Tiger Inn, an old tavern with the address '168 Church Street'. It was accessed by a narrow alleyway known as Cockpit Yard that opened out into a small square at its end. All that remains of the area is now covered by tarmac, and today it serves as the Grape Lane reserved car park. Until the demolitions in the 1950s, a blind fiddle-playing ghost was said to haunt Cockpit Yard (which took its name from a cock-fighting pit that served as entertainment for those drinking at the Tiger Inn and the nearby Crown and Anchor at No. 170). On quiet nights, the residents of the surrounding houses were apparently quite used to the sound of quiet fiddle music being played by a ghostly apparition who always wore bandages over both his eyes. Former residents swore that the ghost could plainly be seen from any upstairs window but that once anyone went outside to take a closer look at the spirit it simply vanished into thin air. No one at the time seemed to know who the ghostly figure was, but research by the relative of one former resident in recent years might cast some light on to the subject.

Blind Jack Metcalf (1717-1810), as he became known, was related to the Metcalfe's of Whitby and became blind at the age of six following a smallpox infection. His life is well-documented and it is known that he was born at Knaresborough on 15 August 1717, the son of a poor horse dealer. Despite his affliction, Jack was ever-resourceful and learned to play the fiddle at an early age, making a living from playing whilst working as a travelling entertainer. He supplemented his income by dealing in horses, gambling, betting on fighting cocks and working as a local guide. Jack in his time was known to be quite a ladies' man and, despite his blindness, had no shortage of women chasing after him. One of these young damsels was Dorothy Benson, the daughter of a publican who at that time was the licensee of the Granby Hotel in Harrogate. Whilst courting the young lass, Jack continued his womanising and inevitably slipped up by making another woman pregnant.

At the insistence of Dorothy, who pledged to stick by him, Jack decided to run away. It is believed that it was during this period he was to be found in the Whitby district: he lodged with an aunt and played his fiddle to earn a crust, probably at the Tiger Inn. In the meantime, in Jack's absence, Dorothy was encouraged by her father to find a husband and to forget about her old beau. Reluctantly, she agreed to marry another local man, and was about to

The Fleece Inn, Thirsk, as it was in the 1800s. It was from here that Peter Elliot, Yorkshire's Blind Horseman, and his team of blind horses ran a regular coach service. Elliot was reputedly a friend of Blind Jack Metcalfe who later went on to haunt Cockpit Yard in Whitby.

seal the partnership when who should turn up to whisk her away but Blind Jack, having walked and hitched rides on farmers' wagons the whole way from Whitby. Without further ado, Jack eloped with Dorothy and made her his wife. She eventually gave birth to four children and died in 1778.

Jack continued to perform feats that would defy any sighted man. He once walked to London to play his fiddle in front of a large audience and then walked back again all the way to Yorkshire. He also succeeded in becoming an assistant to an Army recruiting sergeant during the Jacobite Rebellion of 1745, and in the peace that followed exported Scottish-spun stockings from Aberdeen to England. Ten years later, having carted stone and other goods for a living, he bought a stagecoach – and incredibly drove the coach himself, without apparently any concern being shown amongst his passengers.

If the prospect of a blind man being allowed to drive a public stagecoach seems unlikely, it is interesting to note that there was at least one more blind man with this occupation, called Peter Elliot, who was reputedly an associate of Blind Jack. Elliot gained notoriety as 'Yorkshire's blind coachman'. In truth, Elliot was partially sighted in one eye, but it was said he could scarcely see a yard in front of him. This one-eyed man also favoured one-eyed horses, and incredibly drove a famous team of four horses known as the 'blind uns', the lead horse having a single seeing eye. It is hard to believe that this legendary team of four horses and driver had only two functioning eyes between them, and that under the control of Elliot they drove passengers on the York to Darlington section of the Express London and Newcastle coach route, leaving from the Fleece in Thirsk.

Throughout his life, Blind Jack continued to prove his resourcefulness. With the money he made from coaching he invested in road construction, winning contracts to build around 180 miles of turnpike roads in the northern area (including, it is believed, some in the Whitby district). He went on to live to the ripe old age of ninety-two, and at his death was buried in Spofforth churchyard (he lived in the area at that time) on the 26 April 1819. His spirit, however, appears to have remained in Whitby, and on warm summer nights he entertained the residents of Cockpit Yard with the gentle sound of fiddle playing until his old haunt was finally demolished under slum-clearance plans in the 1950s.

Former Whitby Archives

The former archives building on Grape Lane, just around the corner, was said to be haunted by a number of ghosts, though none of them appeared to wish harm to those who witnessed them; indeed, as far as one can tell, they never even seemed to be aware that they were being observed. Among these were a variety of indistinguishable misty figures that are said to have walked through walls, and a more clearly defined old sailor with a sack over his back that was seen to briskly walk along the basement corridor – only to vanish completely once it has rounded the corner leading into the old boiler room. Mild poltergeist activity has also occurred at various intervals, such as the time when a plastic biro pen lifted itself off an office desk and flew across the room. This was witnessed by two people who were working nearby. Both confessed to being more amused than frightened by the experience.

Electricity Board Headquarters

Way down at the southernmost end of Church Street is a group of modern houses that occupy the site of a former Electricity Board Headquarters, opposite the entrance to Green Lane. This brick-built building was apparently haunted by male figures that could be seen silently passing through doors and walls, carrying planks and ropes. Workers there believe that these were the ghosts of shipyard workers who formerly worked on the site, long before the electricity board's buildings were put there. Two dry docks occupied the site, and it is said that the bow sprits of the sailing ships placed in the docks stretched way across the road and were in danger of breaking the windows of the houses on the far side. Though there is no explanation for the misty figures seen from time to time, it has been speculated that they are indeed the ghosts of former workers who lost their lives whilst occupied in the repairing of various ships over the years.

Whitby Workhouse

On the road now known as the Ropery stands a large building used as business premises. In former days it was a hospital, and before that Whitby Workhouse. In its hospital days – and on later occasions – a number of hauntings were reported in the echoing corridors of the building. Kitchen staff reported hearing ghostly screams, office workers reported phantom footsteps and at least one cleaner is said to have left the building after a frightening experience when a number of screaming figures could be heard coming towards her, accompanied by the shouting of men's voices. When the shouting stopped, a bedraggled woman appeared to float towards her through the door she had hurriedly closed. The cleaner is said to have fled the building, never to return again.

In more modern times, when building work was being undertaken to convert the old hospital into commercial premises, a cavity was found in the north-west wall containing a number of old bones. These were taken for analysis and were found to be of mixed animal origin. It would seem that when the original building was constructed, the builders had placed the bones there for luck, mimicking a more ancient practice where animals were actually sacrificed and eaten during the construction of new buildings. In ancient times, the ritual did indeed include placing bones in a receptacle in the foundations of the north or west wall and mixing the animals' blood with the mortar. Despite advice not to remove the bones from their resting place, the building's owner at that time seemed relieved to be told that the bizarre find was not human in origin and decided to donate them to Whitby Archives Heritage Centre.

Spring Vale

Leading down from the roundabout at the top of Pannett Park is the entrance to Spring Vale (which is now in danger of losing its identity and becoming part of Stakesby Road). There is a lovely little cottage in the dip of the Vale which sits at an angle to the others with its frontage facing towards what were once open fields, but which now look over to Chubb Hill surgery and pharmacy. Those who have lived in the cottage in previous years reported the infrequent presence of a rather gentle ghost in the form of a woman in blue.

She is said to walk silently down the short staircase whenever a happy activity is occurring in the house (such as a family gathering or party). Her appearance is always fleeting and she quickly vanishes at the bottom of the stairway as quickly as she first appeared at the top. The lady in question appears to be quite young and is semi-transparent in nature, and is apparently unaware of those who witness her. Around sixty years ago a young boy was sitting at the bottom of the stairs watching adults as they drank and made merry at a Christmas party in what was his grandmother's house, when he saw the young woman. He asked his uncle, who was standing nearby, who the lady was. His question drew a blank response, as apparently the uncle could see nothing in the direction in which the young lad pointed. Many years later, as an adult, the boy told his ageing grandmother about the incident and received a surprising response: 'What was she wearing?' When told she was wearing a gown similar to a blue negligee, his grandmother put her hand to her mouth. 'Well, isn't that strange?' she replied. 'When I originally bought the house I was told that it was haunted by a woman in blue, but I never saw anything in all the years that I lived there!'

Pannett Park

Exterior ghostly activity is not at all uncommon in the Whitby district. As an example, Pannett Park once had its own ghost in the form of a crying boy aged about twelve years of age. The distressed spirit is said to have been seen regularly in the park at a point where a pair of whalebones once formed an arch. The ghost evidently disappeared forever when the rotting arch was finally removed. Old residents speculated that this pitiful youngster was one of those who lost his life on one of the many whaling ships that used to sail in and out of Whitby. A number of these poor lads are known to have succumbed to the harsh conditions, and many froze to death in the rigging whilst on lookout. One example of a tragedy of this kind involved young Albert Walker, the seventeen-year-old son of local jet merchant Elisha Walker. Other young lads suffered equally terrible fates due to their inexperience – including boys who fell overboard and drowned, or crashed to their death from masts during howling gales – but some have speculated that the ghostly Pannett Park boy may perhaps have suffered a much more bizarre fate.

It was not at all unusual for ships to arrive back in port without the ship's boy, with captains having the distressing task of telling parents that their son had drowned at some period during the voyage or perhaps had died from starvation when a ship had become trapped in ice for months on end. In these harsh circumstances sailors would survive by catching fish or eating bears and seals. Often, however, no food supplies could be found and the will of the sailors to survive starvation would lead to them taking extreme measures: ropes and clothing would be eaten in order to fill stomachs, and the ship's dogs and rats are known to have found their way into the cooking pot on many occasions. Though it was never discussed except in regard to the crews of ships from other ports, and then only in whispers, many of the old sailors knew that in times of extreme hunger the men sometimes resorted to cannibalism – with the youngest member of the crew making a tender morsel for a crew of hungry men. Though undertaken as a last resort, such incidences were not uncommon. Edgar Allen Poe, in his *Narrative of Arthur Gordon Pym*, published in 1837, wrote of a fictitious occurrence of this kind based on a real-life incident.

As another example, in 1884 a murder trial took place of a group of sailors from the English yacht *Mignonette* who, in desperation, had eaten their cabin boy, Richard Parker, after their ship had sunk. The men were eventually tried, found guilty and were each sentenced to death. Luckily for the men concerned, their sentence was later transmuted to a short spell of imprisonment due to

Whitby's West Cliff whalebone arch was one of many to be found in the town in earlier times. This rare photograph shows another one situated in Pannett Park. Locals claimed it was haunted by a weeping boy.

the extreme circumstances in which they had found themselves. In a rare breaking of the sailor's code of secrecy regarding personal experiences of this kind, one of the accused, Tom Dudley, the yacht's captain, confessed, 'I can assure you I shall never forget the sight of my two unfortunate companions over that ghastly meal, we were all like mad wolfs who should get the most, and for men, fathers of children, to commit such a deed we could not have our right reason.' In his book *The Cannibal Within*, Lewis F. Petrinovich reveals similar incidents that he states were all '...in accordance with the proper tradition of the sea'.

Fitz Steps

Other ghosts which haunt Whitby's open spaces include a headless male figure which has been seen wandering up and down Fitz Steps, the short flight of stone stairs on the footpath between Mayfield Road and Ruswarp Fields. His ghost has also been spotted sitting at the water's edge below the old railway viaduct where it was first disturbed by a fox hunt in the early 1900s. No one appears to know who the man is, though he is said to be dressed in military dress from the Civil War period. It has been speculated that he was once a resident of Ruswarp Hall, which has also been the scene of ghostly sightings over the years. Old reports of the ghost say that the man carried his head under his arm, but other reports from more modern sources conflict with this description and say that he only carries

A sometimes headless ghost in period dress is still said to haunt Fitz Steps between Whitby and Ruswarp. The same spectre was once spotted by a local fox-hunting pack and is said to have vanished into the River Esk, pursued by the hounds.

a wide-brimmed feathered hat under his arm. Perhaps there is more than one individual involved in these supernatural sightings?

The Carrs

Hikers walking along the area known as the Carrs between Ruswarp and Whitby have reported seeing a spectral goose flying around the area close to the riverside at dusk, where it squawks and scatters its feathers in an alarming way. Coincidently, this could be connected with the story of a local man who was known to one and all as Goosey. He attracted the nickname after initially losing a bet to eat a whole goose at one sitting: not to be outdone, he attempted the task again and succeeded at a second try. Following the bet, Goosey was found murdered in the River Esk between Ruswarp and Sleights on the same day. His murderer and the motive for his killing were never found.

CHAPTER FIVE

Secrets in Stone

Gargoyles, Chimeras and Gothic Symbols

We watch by day, and by moon glow
See generations born and die
We speak of much to those who know
But few can see us near the sky

(anon)

Few people bother to look upwards towards the roofs and pinnacles of some of Whitby's high buildings, but to fail to do so is to miss hundreds of gargoyles, chimera and other Gothic symbolism to be found there. These symbolic figures and designs were used for a variety of reasons in the distant past, including the transmission of secret messages to 'those with eyes to see', the magical protection of buildings, the depiction of religious messages to those who could not read and as secret signs of faith during times of religious conflict. The interesting thing about these messages from the past is that they interconnect and intertwine with a variety of beliefs ranging from devout Christianity and astrology to Paganism and ancient magic. Surprisingly, figures, symbols and other devices from all these belief systems are to be found alongside each other on old buildings of all kinds and continue to be used subtly by architects in ultra-modern building projects today (e.g. the pyramid at Paris's Louvre gallery). As we will see, ancient Pagan devices are also to be found on Christian churches today, even in Whitby, including representations of the Pagan Green Man figure (though admittedly they might take a little searching for).

Gargoyles in the strictest sense are water spouts, usually in the form of a grotesquely carved face or figure that projects from a building and diverts the water from the roof or drainpipe away from the walls. The word is Latin in origin, *gurgulio*, and means 'throat' – and indeed most, but by no means all, true gargoyles are in the form of an open mouth from which the waste water runs from the building. The Old French word *gargouille* has the same roots as does our English words 'gargle' and 'gurgle'.

Today, almost any carved figure seen upon a building is described as a gargoyle, though those made for purely decorative or symbolic purposes are actually called chimeras, of which there are some excellent examples to be found throughout the town of Whitby. Many are in the form of grotesque humans or creatures, whilst some appear as lifelike carvings. There are also a number of cartoon-like figures, showing that humour was just as much a part of life in former times as it is today.

Gargoyles and chimeras can be found in abundance in Whitby, though often it is necessary to gaze upwards in order to see them. For those wanting to view them in detail, a pair of binoculars is recommended. Two of these winged dragons are to be found at the top of the drainpipes on each side of the NatWest Bank building.

The origins of these curiosities lie in the Middle Ages, when stonemasons were completing projects such as abbeys, castles and churches; gargoyles also saw a resurgence of popularity in Britain and throughout Europe during the building of Victorian neo-Gothic churches. Traditionally it seems that each mason would be allowed to carve gargoyles to his own design. As these often appeared far above the ground where they could not be seen clearly (and there were no telescopes before the late 1500s), liberties were often taken with the designs. There are cases to be found of gargoyles in the shape of figures urinating, picking their noses and even defecating, as at Freiburg Cathedral. Though the builders found great merriment in carving these grotesque Gothic figures, the church authorities would certainly not have been so amused had they known what their stonemasons had been up to. It should be remembered, however, that in most cases gargoyles were added as late finishing touches to completed buildings and as such would be put in position at great height at the last minute before the scaffolding was taken down.

Some gargoyles have definite mystical significance and were obviously ordered by the authorities and placed on the buildings for specific reasons, including those

Chimeras such as these two examples from the West Cliff Congregational Church show the imagination and artistry of the stonemasons that carved them. Though many are grotesque, these two could easily be characters in some Walt Disney fantasy cartoon and seemed to have been put in place to add a touch of humour to the others surrounding them.

put in place as a protective talisman. These will often be grotesque in fashion and will peer down towards the entrance doors as if to keep out the Devil and ward off any evil brought in by those entering the building. Some old churches also had a picture of the Devil carved into the entrance paving stone or steps. The obvious intention here was that everyone who entered or left the church would symbolically walk on the Devil's face. Most medieval buildings have a specially designed gargoyle that is deliberately designed to be in a position where it will catch the first rays of the morning sun.

The parish church of St Mary's, being the oldest in the town, is not, as one might expect, a prime example of symbolic architecture: it sports only a few gargoyles around the perimeter of its tower, and only one is well-preserved. They take the form of identical goggle-eyed human heads with animal ears and gaping mouths and serve as regular roosting spots for the ravens and other birds that fly around the churchyard. Examples of chimera in the form of worn human faces are to be found at the foot of the carved archway around the clock and a couple of human heads flank the Norman doorway in the railed-off section to the eastern corner of the church. Whatever other figures that may or may not have existed have either worn away or been removed. For example, there is a totally unrecognisable figure on the apex of the roof and a carved crowned head on display within the church, though this may have actually come from Whitby Abbey.

This carving is one of the few gargoyles to be found on the parish church. It is also the best preserved and may actually be a replacement put in place at a later date.

The Abbey

Few external examples of carved heads from the abbey survive, though a large torso of a bishop, which may have come from a statue, was found a number of years ago by the owner of nearby Caedmon House whilst excavating a cellar. Also, three figures – which appear to represent either two knights or men in clowns' hats, and another man with Satan-like horns – have been found and cemented into the surrounding walls. They can be seen by walking through the archway at the side of the Abbey House exhibition building. Humans with horns had a double meaning in ancient times and though they were often meant to depict demonic forces, they also represented people who would be discarded by God at the Last Judgement, as allegorically referred to in the Bible parable of the sheep and goats (Matthew 25:31) where readers are told that, 'All the nations will be gathered before him, and he will separate the people one from another as a shepherd separates the sheep from the goats'. The main entrance gates to Abbey House also once had figures upon them – one old document indicates that they were mounted knights – but now all that remains of them is a very worn and unrecognisable carving on top of one of the pillars.

These two well-worn faces (inset) from Whitby Abbey have been cemented into the wall close to Abbey House and can be seen by following the footpath around its perimeter.

Methodist Chapel

Chimera of a different kind can be found on the former Methodist Chapel directly below the abbey and close to the end of Grape Lane in Church Street. This distinctly noticeable religious building was in recent years turned into an Italian restaurant. On its façade, two stone faces with blank, glazed eyes stare down at passers-by. These are probably meant to represent early founders of the Methodist movement, possibly John and Charles Wesley.

Two eyeless faces (above) gaze down from the frontage of the former Methodist Chapel in Church Street. Their high position means that they often go unnoticed by passers-by.

St John's Anglican Church

Across the bridge at the far end of Baxtergate (where it meets Bruswick Street) stands St John's Church. Strangely it doesn't have a single gargoyle, not even one representing St John: indeed there appears to be no carved figures of any kind on the outside of the church. Instead, the church displays another prominent religious symbol signifying Virgo or the Virgin Mary: it takes the form of prominent, odd-shaped *vesica piscis* (fish bladder) windows above its entrance. This simple shape, obtained by the intersection of two circles of the same size (representing the spiritual and material worlds), has a complex mystical symbolism incorporating elements of the Virgin Mary, the female genitals and the birth of Christ. It also has deep mathematical and religious symbolism in that the width to height ratio used in obtaining the shape has been calculated as 265:153. (The number 265 is the nearest whole number to the square root of 3 (another mystical number) whilst 153 is the number of fish miraculously caught by Christ in the Gospel of St John). This same *vesica piscis* symbol has even older pre-Christian connections with birth. Under its alternative name of mandorla (almond seed) it represents any virgin birth (including that of the Pagan virgin Turkish nymph Nana, who was conceived of a child after a ripe almond was nurtured between her breasts).

One of the *vesica piscis* shapes on St John's Church. Far from being just an unusual designed window, the shape is filled with complex mathematical, mystical and religious symbolism and can be found on architecture, both Christian and Pagan, throughout the world.

Though not present in this case, another architectural device often found in old churches features ears of corn. In both Pagan and modern church architecture it also relates to virginity and fecundity, though the reason for this is not always obvious. The explanation lies in the heavenly zodiac where, in the constellation of Virgo, the brightest star is called Spica. Spica means 'ear of corn'. When found in church or mystically symbolic architecture, an ear of corn represents the Virgin Mary (or Virgo). Anyone who has visited medieval churches will have noticed that the virgin is often shown holding an ear or a sheaf of corn, whilst in some depictions her clothing is decorated with the same symbol.

St Hilda's Roman Catholic Church

Across the road from St John's, a mysterious and unusual gargoyle is to be found on the front of the St Hilda's RC Church. It takes the form of a winged lion. This is a common gargoyle on much older buildings, where it often represents the pagan Sun God. On churches, however, a winged lion usually symbolises St Mark, though it can represent 'Christ the King', whose image is linked to the ancient belief that lion cubs are born dead but resurrect to life

Virtually unseen by the vast majority of residents and visitors, the unusual combination of a winged lion at the foot of a pyramid sits way up high on St Hilda's Roman Catholic Church. The conjunction of the two symbols is reminiscent of the Sphinx in Egypt.

after three days. Another medieval belief concerning lions is that they always sleep with their eyes open. Because of this, their image was widely used as a protective device on all kinds of buildings and perimeter fences. Unusually, this figure, the only one on the building, faces south. Under normal circumstances it should have been placed on the east facing wall so as to catch the first rays of the rising sun but, perhaps because of the church's position, the early morning sun is prevented from reaching the eastern wall. It appears that the architect may have placed the gargoyle in a southerly position so that it still absorbs the first rays of the sun that fall upon the front of the church as they emerge from behind the shadow of adjacent buildings.

Few residents or visitors are even aware of this symbolic winged lion and even more fail to recognise that it has been placed at the bottom of a symbolic pyramid. What this pyramid represents is harder to define in this context. One possibility is that it is a symbolic representation of the belief that the priesthood of today stretches back in an unbroken line to the High Priests of Ancient Egypt. The pyramid also represents knowledge, with the highest knowledge being found at the top. In some depictions it contains an 'all seeing eye', representing the greatest powers on earth. This eye is found in Masonic decorations and ceremonial regalia as well as on US banknotes. It is also frequently found in churches in various forms, especially on stained-glass window decorations where it represents the 'eye of god'. Two unusual 'eye' examples in semi-disguised form can be seen at the Templar-related church at Westerdale near Whitby. One appears in a curious stained-glass window hovering above a blue Devil and a depiction of St Matthew accompanied by three zodiac signs. The second all-seeing eye hides behind a multicoloured fish in another window. Incidentally, outside, close to the pathway of this church, is perhaps the only Templar gravestone surviving in the Whitby district.

These two unusual stained-glass windows both contain symbolic eyes, in this case representing the all-seeing eye of God. They are to be found in the village church at Westerdale on lands once held by the Templars. The church still celebrates its historical links with the order.

Brunswick Methodist Church

Moving up Brunswick Street towards Flowergate, pedestrians pass the Brunswick Methodist Church (which is no longer open for services). Like its neighbour, St John's Church, it also appears to have no gargoyles or chimeras; it does, however, have a magnificent carved angel holding a scroll containing a Latin inscription that translates as 'Praise to God'.

United Reformed Church

This church, at the top of Flowergate, also appears at first sight to have no symbolic architecture other than the usual petal-shaped windows, whose numerological significance is related to the Bible. This type of window is common in many churches. Those with four 'petals', known as quatrefoils, represent the four evangelists, Matthew, Mark, Luke and John, whilst the trefoil, with three, indicates the Trinity of God the Father, Son and Holy Ghost. Other numerical combinations have further significance.

They also have numerological messages that transcend religion, and like the architecture of this church convey more than meets the eye. Above the stone porchway, with its pyramid or triangular-shaped top (another representation

Symbolic quatrefoil and trefoil windows, together with four windows set within a dome-shaped frontage, have symbolic significance to those who understand the architect's 'message in stone'.

of the Trinity), is a dome-shaped section containing four arched windows. A modern owl (symbol of wisdom) also stands on top of the entrance, probably put in place to keep other birds off the building rather than to convey any religious or mystical meaning. The significance of the four arches within a dome is explained in Tatarkiewicz's *History of Aesthetics* where he discusses, in rather academic terms, Pagan and early Christian architecture in relation to modern church buildings:

> The influence of the pseudo-Dionysius extended also to architectural details. His concept of emanation inclined the builders to employ a symbolism different from that used before – a multiple symbolism – to symbolize both God and his works in the same building... its dome symbolized the dome of the sky; and the four arches of the dome represented the four corners of the Earth.

Though in this case the writer was discussing interior architecture, the same idea is being employed here on the outside of a building. Incidentally, the same symbolism was used in the design of Saint Edward's coronation crown. It also contains four arches representing 'the four corners of the Earth.' It is interesting to note that the peak of the United Reform Church frontage ends in a similar pyramid shape, which also contains four arches, a symbolism that will not be lost on freemasons as their own Freemason's Lodge on John Street has four arched windows, two of which are placed within an architectural dome shape. The building also has other interesting Masonic symbols on its front wall that are well known to all Freemasons.

West Cliff Congregational Church

Few who pass by this church notice the magnificent display of chimeras that cover the west and north walls, yet the building has stone heads of every conceivable description in abundance. Few churches in the region can match it for the sheer number of symbolic features: look out for life-like human figures of both sexes, crowned kings and princes, a man with a beard, an alchemist with his Phrygian hat, grotesque cartoon-like figures that could have stepped out of a Disney film, an ancient sea captain with a tricorn hat, a medieval merchant, a smiling man with long curly hair and lots of others that stare out from every part of the church walls. Though they are not true gargoyles, a woman with pigtails and a man looking very much like one of the three musketeers sit alongside the very top of one of the church's drainpipes. Binoculars will help in studying this amazing display of chimeras.

Left: At first sight the West Cliff Congregational Church seems fairly unremarkable; however, closer examination reveals an astonishing collection of chimeras in the form of carved faces on both its north- and west-facing walls. **Right:** Faces of every kind stare out from the walls of the Congregational Church including a king, a prince, a sailor and a young woman in pigtails. All are original in design and none appear to be repeated.

St Hilda's Church

A similar type of winged lion to that found on the Roman Catholic church at the bottom of Brunswick Street is to be seen on St Hilda's C of E Church on the West Cliff, though to see it clearly, one really needs a pair of binoculars. In this case it does face directly towards the sunrise. A variety of other symbolic figures can be spotted protruding from various points on the church, including an eagle. Such figures are common on many churches and often include a winged human or an angel, both of which serve as a representative of St Matthew. Mark appears as a lion, whilst John is usually portrayed as an eagle, though he can sometimes also be portrayed as a mythological scorpion. St Luke appears as a bull. These symbols also relate directly to signs of the zodiac, which themselves are sometimes found on old churches and other public buildings.

St Hilda's C of E Church hides a number of secret carvings, including a Pagan Green Man and other grotesque faces, though you will need binoculars in order to see them clearly.

It may seem strange to link Christianity with early Pagan symbolism and the zodiac, but actually this is quite common, even in modern church architecture. If proof is needed, it is only necessary to gaze up at the stone-carved frieze around the south-east corner of the tower of this church. Hidden amongst the row of decorative leafy squares are: an angel reading a book, a Pagan mask-like

The Pagan Green Man
is meant to signify
the continuation of
existence in the form
of a plant growing
from the mouth of a
corpse. It also represents
death and rebirth and
serves to remind us of
Mother Nature's ability
to constantly reproduce
lifeforms through natural
reincarnation.

A winged creature
protrudes from the
church walls. Its face is
ambiguous: could it be
a man, an animal or a
mythical being?

face and a definite and distinct Pagan Green Man. The Green Man represents death and rebirth and, in its true form, always appears with greenery growing from the mouth of the (dead) man. Other figures are waiting to be found on the pinnacles of St Hilda's, but a pair of binoculars is definitely needed to discern exactly what they are.

NatWest Bank

Churches are not the only buildings that carry these messages in stone and some of Whitby's old bank buildings are also rich in chimeras and carved figures. The most prominent of these are the two large griffins which 'guard' the NatWest Bank at the west end of Whitby Bridge. The griffin features regularly in the architecture of Whitby buildings. Both griffins on the bank are intricately carved and hold shields which greet the first rays of the morning

sun. Don't miss the frieze below them containing two large fishes or mythical sea creatures which traditionally represent the zodiac house of Pisces. In this case they are interspersed with a strange square figure with a central spot, star or sun. Strangely, this mysterious shape is also featured on a truncated pillar at Champley's shop in Flowergate. Before leaving the NatWest Bank, look out for the two gargoyles in the form of ugly dragons that sit atop each of the black drainpipes on each side of the main bank frontage. Griffins also feature on the Cholmley coat of arms on the Old Town Hall , a building that is believed to stand on sealed-off ancient vaulted

A selection of carvings from Whitby banks. Top to bottom: lions with shields on the HSBC Bank face the newly risen sun; griffins face the sunrise on the NatWest Bank; a frieze of mysterious symbols combined with fishes, also on the NatWest; and cherubim above HSBC's entrance porch.

The Chomley arms.

cellars below the market place that were once used as a bonded warehouse by the port's customs authorities. The griffin also features in the name of the ancient White Horse and Griffin pub in Church Street.

HSBC Bank

Across the street from the NatWest Bank is another banking house owned by HSBC. In place of the griffins holding shields, observers will notice four lions. They too hold shields and interestingly are also placed so that they face the early morning rays of the sun on its harbourside wall. On the Baxtergate side, the porticoed entrance with a stone balustraded balcony sports a pair of cherubim, also holding a shield which faces towards the sunrise, and a number of carved heads will be found on top of the pillars which support it.

From top to bottom: a winged dragon on the drainpipe at NatWest Bank; faces on the pillars supporting the HSBC's balcony; one of the discreet grotesque faces on the Yorkshire Bank frontage; a mythical figure at the entrance to Barclays Bank.

Yorkshire Bank

Opposite and a little further on from the HSBC is the Yorkshire Bank building. It has a number of mystical symbols which appear to have been purposely hidden from all but those with the keenest eyes. Along the carved freeze on its front wall are a row of square Yorkshire Rose designs carved in stone. However, if you look carefully you will note amongst them a number of grotesque square faces. Though not true 'Green Man' images as they have no foliage growing from their mouths, they are of similar design and probably represents a token effort to place traditional protective figures on the building.

Barclays Bank has no such qualms about showing the creatures that 'guard its portal': above the doorway at 21 Baxtergate is a carved dragon or sea monster on one side, whilst on the other is a human-headed creature with wings and what appears to be a snake's body.

Seacroft Guest House

Such was the fashion for protective amulet devices in the past that many of the old shops and houses in the town copied the churches and other edifices by decorating themselves with mystical images and designs. Though most of them were probably following a fashion or tradition without knowing the real meaning behind the symbols, at least in some cases the building's owner must have been fully aware of the symbolic nature of the figures that they used. The Seacroft Guest House on Crescent Avenue is a fine example of this: though on its ground level the building seems no different from all of the others on the road, a glance at the second floor reveals a particularly fine sculptured head. At first glance this appears to portray a man with long plaited hair, but a closer look reveals the fact that the figure is more likely to be female, particularly as the hair appears to have a coronet consisting of ears of corn. If so, this could, as described in the section about St John's Church, represent the Virgin Mary (or at least the zodiacal Virgo). It would be interesting to know who put the figure in place and whether it was carved especially for the building or came from some older building in the town.

Walking back into town, Moss' Pharmacy in the middle of the Skinner Street has two carved lions near the side window of the shop, whilst Bits and Pizzas, close to the junction of Skinner Street and Flowergate, has an ancient small chimera head on a pillar near its doorway. This chimera – which has a resemblance to Minerva or Athena, the goddess of commerce, wisdom, art, war, and schools – is complemented by another small head around the corner on the same building.

Flowergate is one of the oldest thoroughfares in the town. In medieval times it formed a direct route to the abbey and led to stepping stones across the harbour. Its lowest point, known as Primrose Bank, was once a popular picnic spot, before it became a housing area, then shops that themselves made way for the former

Symbols on business premises. From left to right: one of two lions on Moss Pharmacy, Skinner Street; a swan or pelican on Champley's shop, Flowergate; a fine carving on the frontage of the Seacroft guest house in Crescent Avenue; another lion, this time on the frontage of Zodiac Video, Flowergate; and one of two small chimera on nearby Bits and Pizzas.

Woolworth's store. Stepping stones stretched across the then much shallower harbour from Flowergate and continued through a narrow (now blocked up) archway called Fish Ghaut, before climbing the hill to the abbey. The blocked-off archway can still be seen if one looks across the harbour from St Ann's Staith.

Zodiac Video

A little further down from Bits and Pizzas, on the same side of the street, the Zodiac Video shop has another symbolic device containing a lion: it supports a truncated pillar with a chrysanthemum type flower in its centre. The chrysanthemum symbolically represents long life; it can also be used as a representation of the sun, because in Greek the name chrysanthemum means golden flower. Incidentally, to the left of the lion is a frieze of vine leaves and grapes spanning an archway: this design symbolises the Holy Communion for Christians – and, conversely, moral abandonment amongst the Pagans due to its connection with the Bacchanalian feasts.

Champley's

Continuing down on the same side a symbolic swan supports a truncated pillar on the premises of Champley's. The pillar also contains a square design, possibly representing a Pagan cross within a border and a star within a central circle. This curious symbol is still used today by followers of Wicca and Shamanism as a symbolic reference to the elements contained within a protective circle, a concept used in 'Circle Casting'. Strangely, the same design has been found (without the Pagan cross), on picture rocks created by the North American native Indians. In Whitby, a similar design is also to be found on a frieze on the NatWest Bank. In church architecture the swan is often used as a symbol of hypocrisy because its beautiful white plumage conceals black flesh beneath, though in this case it appears to be plucking its breast, so it may in fact actually be a pelican (An explanation of Pelican symbolism will be found in the section about Bagdale Old Hall).

Across the road is the entrance to Cliff Street which serves as a short cut to Paddock Steps (formerly Playhouse Steps) at whose foot is a building that is both architecturally interesting and mysterious, in that it contains a number of unusual decorative carvings. It also has a large square plaque carrying the date 1888 containing the initials 'R.L'. Its corner bay window is supported by what appears to be a representation of a ship's prow, complete with the figurehead of a naked bearded man. He wears a scull cap and had his lower modesty protected by leaves and foliage. The rest of the building has some complementary foliage and flower panels.

Closer to ground level, beneath the windows are some more decorative panels showing human faces with long hair and beards intertwined with foliage, roses and small birds. The grapes, similar to those on the frieze near Champley's,

Unusual carvings on a building at the foot of Paddock Steps, Cliff Street: a naked man in a cap and cape (above); symbolic imagery from the Cliff Street building (right, top and middle); and comparative carvings from the Pagan Sanctuary of Bel in Syria (right, bottom).

are again a sign of both Holy Communion and Pagan moral abandonment. Another panel design shows a small bird with its beak attempting to grasp a rose whilst it struggles in a swirl of vegetation; or perhaps they could be flames coming from the dragon's mouth. Whether this complex set of carvings are symbolically significant or whether they are purely ornamental is difficult to say, but the artistry and flair shown by its creator is on the whole lost to pedestrians who pass it by without a second glance. The imagery used definitely mimics symbolism used in ancient friezes dating from AD 300 which have been found in the ruins of Diocletian's camp at Palmyra, Syria, especially in the Pagan sanctuary of Bel where they are accompanied by a Hellenic 'egg and dart' motif border. This design can be found throughout Britain in both medieval churches and renaissance architecture. The egg and dart symbolises birth and death, and as such is often found on depictions on funeral urns. When accompanied by intertwined ivy it represents fidelity. All three images are also found in Masonic architecture worldwide, alongside other symbolic images.

8B Cliff Street

A little further along the same street is a very mysterious grotesque face on an archway leading to 8a Cliff Street. Though painted black it has a distinct resemblance to a Pagan Green Man without the greenery growing from its mouth. This figure, which is emphasised by the gorgon-like door knocker, appears to be quite old, and again its origins are shrouded in mystery.

A grotesque devil-like face guards the archway to 8a Cliff Street, a house which also has a gorgon's head for its door knocker.

Streonshalh, the ancient name for Whitby, gives its name to this Gothic-looking building situated at the top of the rise from Cliff Street. To its left is Spion Kop, a high ridge from where visitors can sit on the Dracula Seat and take in panoramic views of the town (including Tate Hill Beach, where Dracula's ship came ashore).

Streonshalh

It is but a short climb up the incline at the end of Cliff Street to the tall, spired building known as Streonshalh. With its distinctive Gothic pinnacled roof it looks, at night, like everybody's image of a Gothic horror film mansion. In its position at the top of Cliff Street its windows look out over the harbour, and it is in close proximity to the grassy bank known as Spion Kop where the Dracula Seat will be found. The inscription on the seat reads:

> The view from this spot inspired Bram Stoker (1847-1912) to use Whitby as the setting of part of his world famous novel DRACULA. This seat was erected by Scarborough Borough Council and the Dracula Society to mark the sixty-eighth anniversary of Stoker's death. April 20th 1980.

Streonshalh is not rich in chimera but does have a mythical lion and two dragons on its frontage. It also hides another strange peculiarity in the form of two sack-shaped stones at the foot of the small hedge near the road. It would be nice to link these to the cargo unloaded from the *Dmitri* which foundered on Tate Hill Beach, an explanation often given by guides as they trace the Dracula trail, but the truth about these odd-shaped stones is probably more mundane. They appear to simply be bags of cement which were placed there during building work and which got wet and set solid before they could be removed.

Seamen's Hospital

On the other side of the river, people passing down lower Church Street cannot help but notice the unusual frontage of the Seamen's Hospital, with its strangely-carved symbols over the main archway entrance. Prior to 1747, the original hospital (actually long-term sheltered accommodation for retired seafarers) was paid for by a toll on all ships passing or using Whitby Harbour. In 1748 the toll system was abolished, and by 1756 the administration of the property in 'Hospitall Yards' was run by a board of Trustees consisting of local ship-owners and masters. The double 'l' in the word 'hospitall' is significant and is medieval in origin, probably indicating the site of a similar institution that was situated here in very early times. It is known that the Knights Templar (and later the Knights Hospitaller), who provided and maintained such hospitals, were active in this area. This link to medieval orders can also be found in the names of two public houses: the Fleece (opposite), and the Bottom House (formerly the Golden Fleece). Both have names that can be linked to the Order of the Golden Fleece, a Templar-style organisation that was founded by Philip the Good, Duke of Burgundy and the Earl of Flanders, but which had widespread connections in Europe, particularly in Spain, Austria and Britain. Though the main Order had a restricted membership mainly drawn from royalty and the aristocracy, it also had numerous knights and other followers under its authority, some of whom ran inns in order to raise funds for the Order's work. The Order of the Golden Fleece was founded on the 10 January 1429 and became one of the most prestigious orders of knighthood in Europe.

It is significant that an ancient monastic hospital was also situated at the lower end of Church Street near Spital Bridge. This may be the same, or an earlier version, of the Hospital of St John The Baptist (again linked to the Hospitallers and possibly earlier to the Templars) whose site can be seen on old Whitby maps in exactly the same area. Further evidence to Templar links are to be found in the harbour area curiously known as 'Abraham's Bosom', a symbolic term once used by the Templar Order to indicate the position of refuge provided by them for converts to the order. The present façade of the Seaman's Hospital incorporates a wealth of symbolic features for those interested in neo-Gothic architecture, revealing much about the meanings for those 'with eyes to see'.

The striking architecture of the Seamen's Hospital in Church Street catches everyone's eye, though its symbolic Gothic architectural symbols are little understood.

Its architect was Sir George Gilbert Scott FRIBA (son of the Reverend Thomas Scott) who was born at Gawcott, Buckinghamshire, in 1811. Scott became a leading figure in the revival of Gothic architecture and was himself fascinated by medieval symbolism.

The building's present façade was constructed in neo-Gothic style in 1842 by Scott's own company, Scott & Moffat. Gilbert Scott used the skills he was to become so famous for and incorporated a number of architectural symbols into the building. Amongst these is the model of the ship to be seen set high on the building. This originally had its top masts lowered, as a sign that, like the inhabitants, the ship was 'out of commission'. Arches and keystones are also prominent around and above the central figure. The alcove in the centre of the building now contains a replica of the ship's figurehead of the *Black Prince*, a locally-owned vessel that was wrecked off Skinningrove in March 1890. The figure is in the form of a Turk or Moor with his arm clasped in a 'sign of fidelity'. It represents both loyalty and devotion and is a sign adapted in various forms in the initiation rites of a number of secret societies. According to an article by Syd Barnett in the *Whitby Gazette* of 13 August 2002, the original figure set in the alcove had been a bare-legged nineteenth-century seaman, possibly also a symbolic initiation reference.

The figure three (the number of arches) is also symbolic, representing, amongst other things, the Holy Trinity. It also has mystical significance and is found in musical works of many composers (including in the works of Leon Battista Alberti) as well as in architecture throughout the world. This symbol can come in many forms including the triangle, three interlaced circles, and, in this case, three arches.

The central arch and the area around the *Black Prince* are full of symbolism. The arch's key stone and the rainbow have direct references to Masonic symbolism, whilst the round ball on a pedestal below it and the scrolled shape to the left and right of the figure's feet are Gothic representations of the earth and the 'nadir of time' respectively. Even more Masonic symbolism linked to the mariners who inhabit the building, the Masonic Royal Ark Mariners and the Templars (reputed guardians of the Ark of the Covenant) can be found in the architecture of the central archway. The central keystone, if viewed upside down, projects below the archway and becomes a symbolic ark, box or tomb.

The Gothic and other symbols included on this building are typical of thousands to be found on ancient churches and civic buildings throughout the world. Once understood they can assist us to 'read' ancient buildings like a book and provide a kind of missing link between a wide variety of disciplines ranging from religious art and architecture to music, secret society symbols – and of course the Gothic culture itself. Look out for: The hypercube [1], which represents time as the 'fourth dimension'. In sacred geometry the fourth dimension is an angle perpendicular to the other three, X, Y, and Z. In this case it is combined with the globe, symbol of the earth, representing the four corners of the earth and the four elements of the earth. The globe [2] also represents the earth, or more correctly earthly existence. It is sometimes replaced by, or placed upon,

a square pedestal which has exactly the same meaning. On the skyline of the building can be seen slightly different globes, this time with an Obelisk upon them, symbolically indicating the powers of the earth and sky combined in total existence. The band found around some of the globes represents the equator.

The Turkish or Moorish figure to be seen on the front of the building is a replica of the ship's figurehead from the wrecked *Black Prince*, which went down off Skinningrove in March 1890. It replaced another earlier figure of a bare-legged nineteenth-century seaman.

As in all things symbolic, it pays to take a closer look than normal at what is being portrayed. The anchor [3] near the central arch has of course a direct relationship to seamen, but it is also identified with St Nicholas in his role as patron saint of seamen. It is also a Christian symbol for hope, salvation and steadfastness. But look carefully – in this case the top section of the anchor on the right is not a rope but a symbolic comet [4], and as such represents the infinite. The keystone [5] is a quite literal symbol of the holding together of things through traumatic times, and like the rainbow [6] has religious, mystical and Masonic connections. The upturned coffin, box or ark [7] beneath the arch serves as a reminder of man's ultimate end (as well as being significant to Royal Arch and Royal Ark Mariner Masons). The cherubim (absent in the design here) will be found in similar architectural representations in churches and give added

The front of the Seamen's Hospital is full of Gothic architectural symbolism. (See text for explanation)

meaning to the shape as representing the Ark of the Covenant. The strange curved shapes are a representation of the nadir [8] of time (the lowest point of our existence, i.e. old age) and as such relate to the aged residents of the building, whilst the triangle shapes represent universality (everything).

Having considered the intense effort put into the design of this building, it is not surprising to discover that Sir George Gilbert Scott, the architect, was responsible for a number of prestigious buildings, including the Martyr's Memorial, Oxford (1841), Brighton College (1848), the Government Home Office and Colonial Offices (1858), The Albert Memorial, London (1862), St Pancras Station, London (1865), Glasgow University (1865) and the Edinburgh Episcopal Cathedral (1867). In 1868 he was appointed Professor of Architecture at the Royal Academy and went on to design many gaols and workhouses as well as significant buildings in the Stoke on Trent potteries region. He and his company were responsible for the design of around 1,000 buildings in total, and carried out restoration work at a number of cathedrals and abbeys, including Chester, Ely, Gloucester, St David's, Worcester, Salisbury, Rochester and Westminster Abbey (where he became chief surveyor in 1849). He was knighted in 1872 and died six years later. It is a mark of his prominence that his body was buried in Westminster Abbey.

The architect responsible for the Seaman's Hospital, Sir George Gilbert Scott. He was appointed professor of architecture at the Royal Academy in 1868 and was responsible for designing many of Britain's major architectural projects.

CHAPTER SIX

Eggs, Funerals and Equinoxes

Curious Customs and Rituals

In Yorkshire &c northwards, some country women doe worship the new moon on their bare knees, kneeling upon an earth fast steane.

(Aubrey's Remaines of Gentilisme and Judaisme, 1686)

The town of Whitby was once so isolated from the rest of the surrounding area that the only safe main 'road' was the seaward route from Whitby Harbour to Hartlepool, hence the great deal of interconnected families from both ports. This isolation was fortunate in that many of the older customs that died out in other parts of the country were still being observed here right up to the outbreak of the First World War, and in some cases even later.

Tradition in Whitby is still very strong, despite the town having been 'pulled by its bootstrings' into the modern world in the last forty years or so. Most members of the older generation will remember a time when a walk through the streets of Whitby saw the town virtually devoid of 'foreigners' (meaning strangers) except during the short summer tourist season. Today Whitby has become a year-round international tourist spot drawing on its links with Dracula, Captain Cook, Scoresby, the *Heartbeat* TV series and a whole string of other television and film programmes, not to mention adverts and music videos that have been filmed in the town.

Batting of the Bluestone

This old custom, which died out in the very early 1950s, was a variation of the old-fashioned 'beating of the bounds' ceremony, whereby parishioners perambulated the border markers of the parish. Each year the local rector, accompanied by schoolchildren from all of the local schools carrying sticks, would trace out the parish boundaries. Children would delight in the 'batting of the bluestone', a strange ceremonial beating of a large blueish stone which once stood near the entrance to the farm next to Whitby Abbey on Abbey Plain. To encourage children to attend, packets of pins, small coins and other trinkets were thrown in the air after the ceremony, upon which all the children would scatter in an attempt to gather them up. Why this particular stone was chosen has been lost to history, but it is known that bluestones have mystical significance and are credited with magical healing properties. They occur in many areas of Britain at religious or mystical sites including Glastonbury and Stonehenge but are not usually natural to those particular areas, having been brought from elsewhere.

Carling Sunday

In Whitby, the eating of large quantities of boiled or fried black carling peas steeped in vinegar was once a common Easter tradition on the Sunday before Palm Sunday. This was known as Carling Sunday (with the following day not surprisingly being referred to as Farting Monday...). Under normal circumstances the carlings were only used as pigeon feed, but on this particular day the ritual preparation and eating of the peas was a widespread occurrence. This tradition was once common all over the North in an area stretching from the Humber to Northern Scotland, but with the onset of the Second World War it began to die out in many places. Here, though, it survived way into the 1960s, and carlings would be made available on the bars of most public houses. These were provided free of charge by publicans for their customers to eat or to take home and housewives would also prepare carlings for their families to eat as snacks. The tradition behind the eating of the peas is lost in antiquity but is believed to have Pagan connections to the dreaded Hindu goddess Kali, an Eastern deity dedicated to death, storms, destruction and all things black. Her cult originated in India but is said to have found favour amongst the early Scots and those living north of the Humber, having been brought to Britain by sailors. In Irish folklore she appears as a witch or hag under the name Cailleach; Irish immigrants, who once lived in Whitby in relatively large numbers, could be another reason why the strange practice of eating black peas existed here on Carling Sunday.

This rather battered image is extremely rare, and shows an early group of Goathland Morris Men. The traditional dancing skills were once taught regularly throughout the district by the late Mr Joe Brown (who even visited Whitby schools during the 1960s in order to pass on the tradition to groups of local children).

Plough Stots and Morris Men

Another set of immigrants to make their way to the Whitby area in even more ancient times were the Vikings. Many of their words survive here as local dialect and remnants of their customs and Pagan rites are to be found in the traditional processions and ceremonial dances of the Plough Stots and Morris Men. Even today these dances are performed in the town and surrounding villages at Easter, and other festivals where men and boys can be seen dancing with ceremonial swords. Though today's dances are pure entertainment, it is said that the conclusion of their dance traditionally entailed the linking of swords around the head of a single 'sacrificial victim' in order to ceremonially cut off his head.

Shear Thursday

Easter was also the traditional time for another custom amongst the farming community in the Whitby district. It was a time when farmers and local residents had an annual haircut and beard trim, 'whether they needed it or not'. On the day before Good Friday, known as Shear Thursday, farm workers of all ages would travel in droves to nearby Malton and would ceremoniously gather together to have their long hair and beards trimmed with sheep shears. Following the 'shorning' a day of general revelry took place, accompanied by fairground festivities, heavy drinking and general merrymaking.

Cattle Rustling

Though the town of Whitby was virtually isolated from the rest of the country until the 1800s, with the only main routes out of the town being by sea, there was of course a network of rough minor roads and pannier men's tracks, though they were impassable in bad weather. They were also dangerous places frequented by robbers, footpads and highwaymen. The rustling of cattle was rife in rural Whitby and, despite the severe penalties metered out to offenders, local farming families were the main culprits. They appear to have continued to steal the cattle of their neighbours with impunity. Many methods were employed to disguise stolen animals – including dying their skins a different colour and even painting patches upon them. Perhaps the cleverest trick employed by the ingenious Yorkshiremen was to strap a hot loaf of bread to each cow's horn and to continue to do this with new hot loaves until the horn was soft and pliable. The rustler would then twist the horn of the animal into a strange shape, making positive identification impossible. Though clever and amusing, such practices carried serious penalties. There is at least one case recorded of a man being hung at Tyburn gallows in London for being found guilty of using this trick to steal a neighbour's cow.

Fishing Superstitions

Like farmers, Whitby's fishing community had its own set of magical and mystical beliefs. Whistling aboard a ship was feared because it might blow up a storm, and most skippers would not allow a woman on board as this was definitely a way of bringing bad luck to the vessel. The word 'pig' was never to be mentioned

The penalties for cattle rustling were severe in the eighteenth century, as this old woodcut shows. Despite this, many local farming families continued to steal their neighbour's animals.

on any ship or boat, though the word 'grunter' was an acceptable alternative. Twiddling the thumbs together was a known antidote for anyone on board who inadvertently uttered the dreaded word. Another superstition that still survives amongst some of the fishing community is the fear of seeing a nun, a priest or a one-eyed person whilst on their way to their fishing boat. To come across such a person is considered a sure sign of bad luck and even disaster at sea. So strong was the belief in former times that certain fishermen would immediately turn round and refuse to go to sea that day for fear of what might befall them if they set sail.

Poking Away a Storm

Another local fishing family ritual found in the town and surrounding coastal villages concerned the poking away of a storm. When what was known as 'lippery weather' suddenly arose, families would continuously poke the fire until the poker got red hot. When the poker began to cool again the process would be repeated. By carrying out this ritual it was believed that no harm would come to any relative that was out at sea during the period of bad weather. Though it was common for wives and children to rush to Whitby pier head when a storm-bound vessel tried to enter over the dangerous harbour bar, none would do so without first ensuring that someone had been left at home to continue poking the fire in this way.

Curing Smallpox

In early times, when the dreaded smallpox struck the Whitby district it was commonly believed was that the colour red was a sure cure, and for those who had come into contact with someone who already had the disease it would impart a certain amount of immunity. Sufferers were wrapped in red cloths

In former times it was believed that wearing red would protect anyone visiting the sickbed of a relative who was suffering from smallpox.

and their surroundings were furnished with everything red (including red bed covers, which were believed to burst the pustules). Red nightshirts and nightcaps were also the order of the day and red drinks, regardless of their medicinal content, were prescribed by physicians as curative mixtures.

Evidently this belief was not only common in Whitby but was widespread throughout Britain and even the world. Kaempfer, in his *History of Japan*, wrote that in earlier days, whenever the Emperor's children came into contact with smallpox, not only were they confined in a room where everything was red, but all visitors to the palace were instructed that they should be dressed in that colour and that the curtains, tablecloths, bedding and eating utensils and drinks should also be red. The belief in the 'Red Cure' was not confined to the uneducated, and it is recorded that up until the English physician Thomas Sydenham proposed a new cure in the early seventeenth century, British medical practitioners regularly used the treatment as a matter of course.

Egg Rolling

Pace Egging, a ceremony involving Whitby children calling door to door demanding boiled eggs at Easter time, has long died out, though the practice of egg rolling is still carried out by individual families today. Traditionally, hard-boiled eggs would be coloured with onion skins, cochineal or broom flowers, though in well-to-do families they were actually covered in gold leaf. These would be decorated either at home or in school and would eventually be rolled down hills (or stairs if the weather was wet) on Easter Monday before being eaten at a family picnic. Tradition states that an egg cannot be eaten until it is cracked by other than a human being. Competitions were often held, with the winner being the one whose egg lasted longest. The custom was widespread well into the 1960s when chocolate eggs had largely replaced the hard-boiled variety, though families today still carry out the tradition (which has experienced a revival in recent years).

Egg Scratching

There are numerous legends surrounding the humble egg, most of them connected with creation myths. Alchemy, folk magic and mythological stories have all been connected to eggs in some way, with many demons, goddesses and traditional heroes having been described as mysteriously having been born, not by natural childbirth, but by emergence from an egg. Eggs also represent rebirth in Pagan and Christian belief, especially at Easter time, and in Whitby the eggs would be scratched with pictures and mysterious symbols. This practice survived as a kind of folk-art way into the early 1960s (by which time both children and their parents had long since forgotten the meaning of the strange scratched markings that had been handed down from generation to generation).

Some believe the marks scratched on the eggs, together with the application of gold leaf is a leftover from the ancient alchemical belief in the 'The Philosopher's Egg' used to produce the 'Philosopher's Stone'. The 'Stone' – which itself could turn all base metals into gold – was actually an egg-shaped crucible. It symbolised the four elements necessary for the alchemist to perform his magic art. Earth was represented by the shell and water by the egg white. Fire was indicated by the yolk and air was symbolised by the air around the inner membrane. This alchemical imagery is almost certainly linked to a riddle which was once posed to local children at Easter: 'Earth, Fire, Water and Air, What is the strangest birth under the sun? It leaves the womb, though life has not yet begun; it silently enters the world and yet is seen by none'. The answer was, of course, an egg.

Vernal Equinox

Another common but strange belief relating to eggs in Whitby was that a fresh egg could be stood on its end during the Vernal Equinox (20 March). The conviction was apparently based on the belief that during the equinox the sun's position between the North and South Poles meant that not only was the length of day and night both of equal length but that because of this natural equilibrium few things could fall over on the first day of Spring. This belief links directly back to Pagan times when this same equinox was also known as Oestar, Eostre and the Day of Equilibrium, a time when everything – including our personal feelings, work, rest and play and our physical and mental faculties – were all mystically in perfect balance. Eostre was of course, like the egg, connected to birth and fertility, being that she was the Pagan goddess of fertility and spring, and as such gave her name to the Christianised festival of spring known as Easter as well as to the fertility hormone Oestrogen.

Egg Tapping

As a final example of the strange local customs connected with eggs, we have only to look once more towards Whitby rural communities, where egg tapping is still used by older farmers as a means of keeping eggs fresh. The practice was once common and involved giving each newly laid egg a smart tap or a pin prick in order to damage the base. Historically it was believed that the Devil or evil spirits could inhabit an egg and make it bad, providing it was sealed, but by making a hole in the bottom, his occupation of the space within the egg was prevented. Surprisingly, eggs would be stored in this damaged condition for quite some time in the firm belief that they would stay fresh and good to eat.

Child Vowing

Childless couples in the Whitby district (and perhaps throughout the country) would, at one time, as a desperate measure visit a local church, a holy well or other sacred place to 'vow a vow'. This 'Child Vowing' ritual entailed either praying or carrying out some sacred rite. It would vary from area to area, but in all cases it concluded with a vow that the couple in question would dedicate their first child to God if their inability to have children was taken away. Many country clergymen and nuns are said to have taken to a religious lifestyle because of vows made in this way by their parents, and the custom is said to have clung on well into the twentieth century, despite modern methods of aiding childless couples. If the couple in question were not church-going people, the same ritual would be enacted in a 'sacred' part of a wood or on a very high hill at the time of a new moon.

New Moons and High Places

The new moon and high places had a special pagan significance to many local families and their reverence to both appears to be a survival of the pagan worship of Diana (also known as Artemis), the Moon goddess. Similarly, great reverence was given to conducting various rituals under a new moon, or better still near a smooth lake viewed by moonlight on a still, clear night. Such a lake would be referred to as 'Diana's Mirror'. High places have always had a mystical significance to ancient people and it will be noted throughout the country that churches, castles and hermitages were often built on high places and were usually dedicated to St Michael (who is the patron saint of high places).

St Michael's Mount (Cornwall), Mont San Michelle (France) and St Michael's Chapel on Glastonbury Torr are just a few examples showing that the idea was commonplace throughout Europe, though conversely, St Michael's Church in Whitby (now demolished) was situated low down, close to the River Esk on Church Street.

Diana, also known as Artemis, can be found in various depictions throughout the world. In all cases she appears as a moon goddess and in North Yorkshire was invoked during ceremonies which took place at the new moon.

Christmas and New Year Customs

During Christmas and New Year (or Yuletide, as it was then known) there were once many ancient customs that took place throughout the town. Sadly most have now died out. The Yule log, otherwise known as the Yu Block, Yu Batch or Yule Block, was collected around Christmas Eve and consisted of a large, dry, old tree stump which, it was intended, would burn throughout the Christmas celebrations. In 1686, John Aubrey reported that not only did people sing carols but 'they doe dance and cry, 'Yole, Yole, Yole'. Oak logs were laid in the hearth to burn away slowly throughout the year beneath other fires built upon them and when they were eventually reduced to ashes they were ritually spread on crops in order to spur their growth.

Candles have of course always been associated with Christmas, and in Whitby it was traditional for local grocers in the town to give away long burning Yule candles to their customers at this time of year. The antiquary, John Brand, tells of an ancient custom which involved the lighting of these giant candles on Christmas Eve. '...so as to turn night into day'. Both the candles and the Yule log itself were usually lit with the fragment of an old Yule log and it was generally considered unlucky to use any other method of lighting them. Quite often, frantic activity took place on Christmas Eve as Whitby housewives desperately sought someone who had a remnant of last year's Yule log with which to kindle their own fire. Once lit, the fire would be kept burning throughout the twelve days of Christmas.

Gingerbread

It was also traditional throughout the Christmas season to keep gingerbread and wine handy on a tray close to the front door. This was for the families and individuals who would walk from house to house where they would be made welcome at every call. The gingerbread at that time was home made and was of a dark, dry and much more substantial nature than its modern counterparts. Recipes were closely guarded in families, and unfortunately because of this the methods for making many of the very tasty varieties have been lost forever. Though the practice of whole families calling from door to door largely died out by the 1950s, it is still occasionally carried on at the present time by a few traditionalists in the town.

Merry Christmassing

Carol singing was of course common in the town and so was Merry Christmassing. This involved groups of children calling from door to door after midnight to be the first to wish various householders, including people they did not know, a Merry Christmas. The children would expect a small gift, a mince pie or money, and usually this was freely given. Sometimes the children would be greeted by an astonished newcomer to the district who couldn't understand why these small children, who were complete strangers, were knocking on his door to wish him season's greetings after midnight when they should have been long since tucked up in bed. Generally an explanation of the local custom resulted in the expected gift though children who arrived at a house where 'Merry Christmassers' had already called would be very lucky indeed to obtain anything. Instead, they were generally greeted by another short familiar traditional call, usually through the closed door, 'They've already been!'

The loss of this ancient practice is extremely sad and it is perhaps a reflection on our modern times that in those days (up to the 1960s) the world was a much safer place than at present for all children. It is now astonishing to think that small children would wander around town in the dead of night in what were poorly lit streets to call at the doors of total strangers, yet it was considered completely safe for parents to let their youngsters roam freely in this way without any fear of either harm to their offspring or disgruntled condemnation from concerned neighbours.

First Footers

Happy New Yearing was a similar practice to 'Merry Christmassing', and it took place just after midnight in a similar way on the first of January. If the child had dark hair and was male, this was particularly fortunate because many households awaited the arrival of a lucky 'First Footer' to be the first person to step over the threshold in the New Year.

Black was a significant colour during this ritual and many people dressed up for the occasion in dark clothes, carrying coal and even blacking up their faces with soot. Though in some households a dark First Footer was preferable, all who came to the door were made welcome. However, if the resident was a strict traditionalist or was particularly superstitious, callers would be kept waiting at the door until a first footer could be found who would fit the dark requirements. This involved being male, dark haired and with the necessary piece of coal or Whitby jet upon him. If necessary the coal or jet would be supplied by the householder themselves after which the First Footer and any waiting callers were finally allowed over the doorstep for a celebratory drink.

Robins

Good and bad luck could be brought about by a variety of actions and objects in the minds of old Whitby residents. Though most of us welcome the red-breasted robins to our gardens in winter, country folk here once viewed the 'unlucky' bird with great dread. Even today there are farmers who would rather have a fox than a robin on their land and who will even turn off a television showing a robin. This superstition extends to the ritualistic examination of Christmas cards as they arrive through the letterbox at Christmas time. Any that have a picture of a robin upon them are singled out. Without a second thought a pair of scissors is taken from the drawer and the offending unlucky bird is unceremoniously cut out. It is a strange sight indeed to visit a country farmhouse bedecked for the Christmas season and to see the cards all neatly stacked on the mantelpiece, those which once had a robin upon them conspicuous by the neat hole showing the position where the bird has been cut out and thrown on the fire.

Funeral Customs

The funeral tea which now often takes place after a death has developed from the once commonly held 'wakes'. Relatives in Whitby would commonly stay awake all night beside the coffin which might, according to the wishes of the family, be either open or closed. Though this vigil was traditionally to prevent evil spirits entering the corpse before daylight, in other areas of the country it had a more practical purpose, namely to protect the body being stolen for medical research.

Wakes were common in Whitby in earlier times. At this one, depicted by the artist William Hogarth (1697-1764) in his work *A Harlot's Progress*, the mourners consist mainly of women and a single child.

In 1620 a gentleman recorded that in his father's youth a 'wake song' was sung throughout the night. This was considered a cross between a kind of musical protective charm and a hymn. In the late 1600s a wake was known as a 'watch' in Whitby and was a very common practice. Candles would be lit around the open coffin and a small container of salt would be placed upon the chest of the corpse itself. All clocks would be stopped, mirrors in the house would be covered and the curtains of all windows would be firmly drawn shut. In some families it was the practice to tie the toes of the corpse together with red ribbon. In even earlier times it was said to be unlucky for any animal, insect or bird to enter the room where a corpse was laid in a coffin as it was believed that the Devil could use the animal to get access to the person's soul. Consequently it was a tradition to kill any animal, bird or insect that inadvertently entered the room in which the corpse was laid – even, it seems, to the extent of slaughtering the family pet. The activities that took place at a wake or watch varied greatly depending upon individual family's customs. Prayers, card playing and drinking and smoking were common and it is said that a number of families of Irish origin who had settled in the town during the period of the great potato famine would often hold a full-blown party in the room where the deceased's coffin, open, would take pride of place. Though such 'celebrations' may seem unusual to our modern minds, they were commonplace and were all part of the general belief that if the dead person was left unattended, his soul would be taken by the Devil.

Beseeching the Lop

Earlier in the 1600s it was recorded that mourners 'have mimical playes, sports, e.g. they choose a judge, then the suppliants having first blacked their hands by rubbing it under the bottom of a potte, beseech his lop.'

This custom of 'beseeching his lop', otherwise known as blacking the face of the corpse, may seem indelicate to modern minds but was based on a superstitious belief that such an action would prove that nobody in the room had played any part in the person's death. However if, on the contrary, any dark deeds had taken place leading to the person's decease then it was believed that the black soot placed on the corpse's face by the guilty person would turn red, causing the corpse to bleed.

Sin Eating

At daybreak, following the wake, the danger of the Devil entering the corpse was considered over and it was time for a sin eater to play his part in the funeral arrangements. Sin Eaters were employed by families in order to speed their dear departed on his or her way. These people were usually extremely poor people or even down and outs brought off the street who agreed to eat and drink at the funeral. The idea was that they would assist the dead person in getting to heaven by taking on their lifetime's sins and errors so that his or her soul could pass to the heavenly gates without further hindrance. Records of sin eaters go back as far as the sixth century when part of their duty was, immediately after the sin-eating ritual had taken place, to throw a purple thread known as a 'kop' into a fast-running river to rid the sin eater himself of the dead person's sins. Perhaps this is where the expression 'Cop-out' comes from!

Tom-O-Bedlams

Whitby people were on the whole extremely charitable to poor people in the eighteenth century, though habitual begging by a stranger was definitely looked down upon. It was common practice in many parishes to take beggars to court or to have them transported to the edge of the next parish. Many of these poor individuals in the 1700s were known as 'Tom-O-Bedlams' or ' Tommoes', and were a special type of beggar who had been released from mental asylums under the social reforms of the time. These harmless but wretched people were licensed to beg and were identifiable by a four-inch painted 'armilla' made of tin that identified the individual using numbers or symbols. Like a modern tagging device, the armilla was affixed to their arm so that it could not be removed. In addition these beggars carried a drinking horn around their necks which sympathisers could fill with small beer or other drinks if they so wished.

This kind of beggar was particularly unwelcome in the town as they would often travel in bands and carry whistles or bells which they would sound noisily so as to announce their arrival. The popular nursery rhyme, 'Hark, Hark, the dogs do bark, the beggars are coming to town. Some in rags and some in bags and some in velvet gowns,' is a reminder of those days. The mention of velvet gowns refers to gangs of impostors who travelled the country, and who in effect jumped on the begging bandwagon, often amassing large amounts of money from their activities.

CHAPTER SEVEN

Social Sorcery

Witchcraft and Wizardry in Whitby and District

From Witches and Wizards and magic spells
From things that creep and scratch in the night
From crawling creatures that rattle hedge bottoms
Good Lord deliver us all
Five, Seven, Nine, Eleven

(Traditional)

In Whitby and throughout Yorkshire adults and children would once recite the above verse over and over in order to take their minds off what was worrying them or to give them comfort and a sense of wellbeing when going to sleep (or perhaps when travelling through unlit areas at night). Many people apparently gave great credence to the verse's protective powers, though is difficult to know whether it was considered by them to be a protective magic spell or a religious prayer. Perhaps the invocation of God's name together with the recitation of magic numbers was meant to cover all possibilities.

As in many areas, the belief in witchcraft existed in Whitby and the surrounding area up until the time of the First World War, and indeed survived in pockets of the surrounding county until long afterwards.

A popular spell which was sold at Whitby in the 1600s found favour amongst the local farmers who travelled to market each week, often on foot. Its purpose was to bewitch any walking staff carried by the person who bought the spell and so keep them safe on their journeys:

> Gather on the morning of All Saints Day, a strong willow staff and deeply hollow out its base by removing the pith. Now gather two eyes from a young wolf, the heart and tongue of a dog, the skin from a lizard, a dead spider, the heart of a swallow and a dead bee. Sprinkle with saltpetre and dry between sheets of brown paper in the sun. Gather also leaves of vervain and dry similarly. It be best if these are gathered on the eve of St John the Baptist. If this is not possible then witchwood leaves will suffice. When all are thoroughly dried, grind together and fill the hole in the staff with the mixture. This will protect the traveller from any ill that might befall him on his way.

The eyes of the wolf were supposed to protect the traveller from attack by the animal; the dog's heart and tongue would similarly protect from dog bites and rabies. The lizard and spider, it was thought, would shield the traveller from bites from anything that crawled, whilst the swallow's heart and the dead bee would ensure that no harm came from the air or from stings. Vervain and witchwood (rowan leaves) were a common trusted antidote against the spells of witches. A similar recipe for the staffs of pilgrims was quoted by Shaw Jeffrey in his book, *Whitby Lore & Legend* (1923).

Though acts of sorcery are recorded way back in history, it only became a crime in Britain in 1542 when the practicing of witchcraft and sorcery was treated as a felony, a minor crime punishable by confiscation of possessions.

Belief in witchcraft continued in the rural areas surrounding Whitby up until fairly modern times. Punishments in this area were generally minor, such as the accused being dipped in the village pond.

In 1563 the crime of causing illness by witchcraft was punishable by being placed in a pillory or stocks and/or a year's imprisonment. This penalty was still supported by the Bishop of York, Edmund Grindale, when he came to power seven years later. Under that same law of 1563, a witch who was convicted of causing death using her magic powers was subject to the death penalty. In reality, these laws appear to have been little used in Whitby or in its surrounding areas where witches and wise men were generally respected as part of the social order. In the seventy or so years following on from 1567, the church courts record only a hundred or so cases, most of them minor in nature. Prosecutions often involved 'white witches' who claimed to be able to tell fortunes, find lost objects or cure minor illnesses. Punishment for these 'crimes' were usually trifling in nature: these would range from a complete discharge based on a promise to cease all 'magical' activities to being made to walk backwards through a church congregation wearing only an under-slip whilst confessing their culpability. A few were made to pay monetary fines, but ducking in the village pond or being pelted with apples was also common. Surprisingly some were made to carry out what was one of the earliest forms of community service by helping those in the community less fortunate than themselves.

Despite this, a number of women were executed for crimes of witchcraft in Yorkshire, and there are also records of people who took the law into their own hands and were themselves hung for their part in the killing of witches. One such case occurred in 1667 when three men were hung at York for the murder of a supposed Wakefield witch. By the 1700s there was still a strong belief in witchcraft, but many others dismissed sorcery as a figment of the imagination of uneducated country folk. In 1736, common sense ruled over hysteria and the witchcraft statutes were repealed altogether.

The urban township of Whitby has hardly any recorded cases of witchcraft activity, though the farmers' market is often mentioned as the haunt of various women who were considered witches. In surrounding rural communities the local witch or wise-woman (or in some cases, wise-man) continued to be a respected and sometimes a feared member of the community well into the 1900s. The reason for this is not hard to understand: protection against little understood forces (which people believed manifested themselves as disease, crop failures and runs of bad luck) meant that there was a ready market in such areas for spells, amulets and potions. It was not uncommon for witch posts carved with signs and symbols to be built into the structure of country cottages, whilst witch-stones (natural smooth stones full of holes) would be hung in barns to protect the farmer's animals from evil powers. The last witch post to be discovered in Whitby was in a farm cottage situated near what are now the gates of Whitby Football Club in Upgang Lane. It was formerly surrounded by a number of low-growing rowan trees. The building was in recent years converted and has now become the site of the Jehovah's Witnesses Kingdom Hall.

Rowan trees, also known as Witchwood or Wiccan Wood, were believed to have special protective magical properties and were regularly planted in gardens, often next to the main doorway where they were believed to be a sure defence against the power of witches. The plant vervain was also credited with similar powers. Even the clergy were not immune from these often strong beliefs in witchcraft and sorcery.

It was a common practice until the 1800s on St Helen's Day (2 May, also known as Witchwood Day), to decorate St Helen's Chapel, a small church that was once situated at the bottom of the 199 steps, with branches from the rowan tree that were intended to protect the church from evil influences. After the service was over, sprigs would be taken home by members of the congregation to be hung on the walls of their dwellings as a protection for the general household. From these small branches, even smaller pieces would be broken off and made into an object that would be carried in the pocket or purse as an individual protection against evil spells and magic forces.

The way in which each man or woman gained a reputation as a witch varied from parish to parish. Some individuals achieved the title simply through recognition of their special skills or powers, often because they were accomplished herbalists or they could cast spells (i.e. write prescriptions). Others had a good knowledge of astronomy or meteorology. Such skills enabled the witch to give advice on all manner of things including the curing of ills, the planting or gathering of crops based on weather patterns and making predictions based on seasonal changes. Some were born into families that had a long reputation of having magical powers. These families often passed on their closely guarded recipes, spells and reputations from one generation to another. Special mystical powers were also believed to be inherent in a seventh son. The name Septimus, a once common name in Whitby, was invariably given to such males. Females with similar powers were often nicknamed 'Nanny'.

Though many of these witches' powers were purely imaginary, others were undoubtedly based on genuine knowledge: the ability to read and write, for example, was itself considered to be a magical gift. In an illiterate age when few knew what writing was, it is easy to see how a literate person who was knowledgeable in botany and chemistry could use their power to create a 'spell' by simply writing a herbal prescription. This 'spell' would be seen by the 'patient' as merely a collection of strange magical symbols on a piece of parchment or cloth. Imagine the patient's surprise and wonder when this 'spell' was given to another witch who could not only read the magical marks, but could also use them to make up a 'magic potion' of medicine that would cure or relieve the patient of their toothache, rash, constant headache or similar affliction.

It should be remembered that witches did not always meet our traditional image of an old crone sitting near a fireplace with her 'familiar'. Many were young people – or even men. Some were indeed older women who had built up a reputation over the years and who held a very powerful place in their local society. It was in the commercial interest of such people to bolster the general beliefs of their neighbours and to continue acting in a way that gave the appearance that they had extensive supernatural powers.

Witches, wise women and wise men must have existed in nearly every village in one form or another, though the majority have not been recorded. Stories of those that have been written down often need to be 'taken with a pinch of salt', though they do provide us with rudimentary records of real people who were once considered to be real-life witches. Their stories have left us with a brief glimpse of the lifestyles of the people of the time and in doing so have contributed to the continuing history and folklore of the Whitby district.

Today the village of Ruswarp, though now virtually a suburb, is still quite a small and compact place, retaining much of its village character despite modern housing having been built on the site of the old Ruswarp Mill and a string of houses joining Ruswarp with its larger neighbour Whitby. In the 1800s Ruswarp was even smaller, with a very closely knit community among its tiny population. The exception to this rule was a middle-aged woman known only as Old Katty. She was regarded by all as a malevolent witch who was to be avoided at all costs. None would pass her in the street without crossing themselves and if she was spotted at a distance, the person in question would cross the road or turn back and hurry home in fear. Katty's one and only visitor was a pack-horseman who delivered goods to businesses and residents in the district. Each time he reached Katty's house opposite the mill he would be seen to tie up his horse and to walk into her home without even knocking on the door.

It was agreed that Abe Rogers, the pack-man, wasn't himself a witch so there was much speculation as to how and why he was immune to the witch's powers. Though he was asked on many occasions how he managed to avoid her evil eye, he would not reveal the secret of his power over Old Katty and would answer all such enquiries with a simple knowing smile. The most believed story of the time was that Abe Rogers had come across Old Katty on a moorland path and that neither would give way to the other. Taking a knife from her black

The former Ruswarp Mill is shown here in earlier times. Directly opposite lived Old Katty, an old crone who was feared by all who lived in the village.

gown, Katty had tried to kill the pack-man, only to be thrown to the ground by him and restrained. Old Katty had then resorted to more magic, screaming and chanting until a group of ugly black imps had sprung from the heather ready to attack Abe at the first opportunity. Abe however, being a man of the world, carried protection against just this sort of incident and quickly opened his money bag, scattering some magic rowan powder that he had purchased some time earlier from a magician at a country fair. The magic powder had caused an instant whirlwind which upturned everything that lay loose on the grounds – including fine grit which temporarily blinded Old Katty and disabled her imps. Taking the weapon with which Katty had tried to kill him Abe had cut off the ears of the imps and sent them packing back to the place from whence they had come. From this point onwards, Katty had been in fear of Abe and in order to placate him had offered to feed him and give him a drink whenever he passed her door.

Interesting as this accepted version of events is, it has been speculated by modern historians that Abe Rogers may have actually been the brother of Old Katty or even an old boyfriend who called whenever he was in the neighbourhood. In the superstitious days of the early nineteenth century, it is evident that the locals had their own ideas of how the pack-man had gained his power over the old witch, but who knows? Perhaps Old Katty and Abe gained great pleasure from continuing the mystery and perhaps often shared a laugh over the fantastic stories that had been concocted about their magical relationship.

Susan Ambler of Stokesley was said to have Whitby family connections and was often to be seen at Whitby's Saturday farmers' market. She obtained regional notoriety after a legal hearing took place in 1699 where she was accused of placing a spell on the sheep flock owned by a Mr Adam Clark. Susan, it was said, had enchanted the farm animals causing nine black sheep to be born: she was whipped for her crime. The unfortunate woman was also blamed for the low general birth rate of the flock, as only forty lambs had been born in the whole year. For this additional enchantment, she was ordered to be punished by being placed in the ducking stool and was publicly and repeatedly dunked in the village pond.

Ann Allen was another notorious local witch. In 1780 she was particularly feared by local farmers who believed that she had a particular influence on farming activities, so much so that in the nearby village of Ugthorpe a group of farmers from the Whitby district met to discuss her activities. Rumours had been circulating about the condition of local sheep and pigs that were visibly getting thinner by the day, and of cows that were ceasing to produce milk. Many thought that Ann Allen had put a spell on their flocks, particularly as she kept a number of pigs herself that were all apparently fat and healthy. It was agreed at the meeting that a watch would be put on the woman and that the local priest would be contacted to see what could be done about Ann and her dabbling in the Devil's work. The local priest was either superstitiously gullible or exceedingly crafty, perhaps both, for he informed the men that he too had

had his suspicions about Ann Allen. He told them that in his opinion the Devil was holding the cows by their tails, stopping them eating and holding back their milk supply. He announced that he would say a special Mass to ask God to send an angel to disperse the Devil. For this he would need to be paid an agreed sum by each farmer. He assured them that a positive result was guaranteed, particularly if each farmer would say three paternosters and three Ave Marias each night over their skeels [milking buckets]. It appears that the farmers, though superstitious, were not entirely stupid. Being Yorkshiremen, they were also keen to hang on to their hard-earned cash, and were not at all happy with the priest's suggestion; consequently, it didn't take long for them to agree to turn down the priest's offer of a special Mass. Though they were undoubtedly reluctant to lose their cattle and milk supply, they were certainly not prepared to lose their hard-earned cash as well!

This was not the end of the story though: the matter came to a head when another farmer who had not attended the original meeting suddenly found that his cattle were also beginning to suffer and were supplying less and less milk as the days went by. In a fit of temper, the man, followed by a party of curious neighbours, headed for Ann Allen's house where a furious row took place. The farmer accused Ann of secretly milking his cows by magic means. Ann, of course, denied the charges, but could not answer the question as to why she had a milking stool in her kitchen when she only kept pigs for a living. In a blind fury the angry farmer picked up the three-legged stool and threw it at her, hitting her across the head and knocking her to the floor. The story from this point appears to have suffered from years and years of enhancement in the re-telling, as legend goes on to tell us how milk began running from the broken leg of the stool and continued to do so every time the name of a sick cow was uttered. In reality, the story was probably less dramatic: Ann may have been guilty of secretly milking other people's cows at night. Whatever the truth, she was found guilty of bewitchment and was punished by being paraded three times through the village dressed only in her sark [nightdress] as a penance. The stool, we are told, was ceremoniously burned upon a bonfire set up on a plot of land situated near to Ugthorpe Mill where witches were reputed to dance on All Hallows Eve.

Around 1780 a strange case of a church-going Roman Catholic witch was recorded in Goathland, a small local village better known to the nation as Aidensfield in the *Heartbeat* TV series. Nanny Pierson, a reputed sorcerer, would call each day at the farm of a Mrs Webster, leaving an empty milk jug and picking up a free full one. The inference was that by providing the witch with free milk, the farmer and his wife would suffer no ill effects from her magic. On one occasion, a goose owned by Mrs Webster was sitting on its eggs in a warm place near the farm chimney-stack and took exception to the visit of old Nanny Pierson, going berserk and breaking a number of its eggs in the process. For no reason whatsoever the goose continued to react in this way every time old Nanny appeared on subsequent visits. Mrs Webster discussed the matter with her husband, who began to wonder whether the local witch had placed a spell on it. Luckily for the farmer's wife, a visiting male witch known only as the Wise Man of Scarborough was in the district doing his rounds. When he called at the Webster farm to ask if there was anything he could do to bring the occupants good fortune, Mrs Webster told him the tale of Nanny Pierson's visits and asked him for a solution to the problems with her goose.

The woman was told to procure some holy water from the local Roman Catholic priest and was instructed that she should place it in Nanny Pierson's milk jug, pouring milk on top of it to disguise its presence so as to break the Goathland witch's spell. When Nanny Pierson next came to collect her milk, the spell had been set and appeared to work immediately. The goose flew at the woman, dashing the jug from her grip and smashing it on the milk parlour floor. The witch fled in terror.

It is said that Nanny Pierson vowed never to visit the farm again until the bad-tempered goose had left. Mrs Webster, however, was quite satisfied with this arrangement and believed that the magic spell had done its work. She swore that the power of the wise man far outweighed that of the local witch, and Nanny Pierson immediately lost a lot of credibility in her local community.

It would seem that a power struggle was going on in the village between Nanny Pierson and the visiting wiseman – who, it appears, could have also been in collusion with the local priest, considering that the cleric was making a tidy sum from the selling of holy water for the wiseman's spells. This is illustrated by another incident in which a local landowner is said to have consulted Nanny Pierson to obtain a spell or potion that would make his daughter fall out of love with a common farm-hand she had become romantically attached to. Nanny administered a potion to the young woman who quickly became paralysed from the waist down. Alarmed at the result of his and the witch's actions, the landowner immediately turned to the Scarborough Wiseman to ask him to reverse the spell that Nanny Pierson seemed unable to put right herself. The wiseman said that he would be unable to affect a cure unless he could be given some of Nanny Pierson's blood which he would mix with holy water purchased from the local priest so as to make an ointment. Shocked at the thought that he was being asked to kill the witch, the girl's father said fearfully that he did not wish to end up on the gallows at York.

The wiseman assured him that there was another magical solution and gave him a date some days in the future when he said that all witches habitually shape-shifted. The man was told to go out that night near Nanny Pierson's home and to kill a hare which was sure to be Nanny Pierson in disguise. Though the hare would die, Nanny would escape to live another day and the necessary blood could be collected from the animal's corpse to be placed in the magical ointment. Legend tells us that following the treatment, the young woman did gradually recover from her paralysis. Nanny Pierson reputedly gave up witchcraft and turned back to her Roman Catholic religion, refusing to carry out any further acts of magic for the villagers.

Sally Akers was a Whitby-born witch with a kindly personality who lived at nearby Egton. She studied astrology and made a steady income by predicting auspicious days on which to hold weddings and Christening services. Her 'wedding florins' found a ready sale amongst local couples who had previously consulted her concerning the naming of a lucky day upon which to tie the marital knot. For a florin (2 shillings), a tidy amount in the 1780s, Sally presented them with a 'wedding charm' consisting of a lead disc which she had made herself using a clay mould. Each disc carried the name or initials of the couple together with their wedding date on one side, and a number of astrological or alchemical symbols on the other. Major J. Fairfax Blakeborough, a member of the local gentry, wrote in 1880 that he had a number of these florins in his possession. He described them as having signs of the zodiac clearly marked on one side, together with the initials of the happy pair and the date of marriage. Others were illustrated with three interlaced rings or a triangle representing the sign of the trinity. Many also had double hearts representing the love of the happy couple.

Another of the area's respected witches was Molly Milburn of Danby. Molly Milburn lived during the late 1600s and was known by one and all as 'The Enchantress'. Her speciality was using silk thread to carefully embroider animal skins with spells, signs of the zodiac and other symbols. These talismans, once officially enchanted by Molly Milburn, were prized by local people (who believed that they brought them good luck). The ornamental items would also ward off the evil eye and were said to cure a great variety of illnesses. Among the symbols used by her was the old cladach (originally a more sexually explicit depiction involving two hands and the female genitals but represented in the modern form by a pair of clasped hands and a heart). Lover's knots and hearts were also used to decorate a love talisman, whilst depictions of acorns were said to ensure strength and a long and happy life for those that were ill. Various kinds of circular rings were embroidered to signify eternity; sun symbols ensured that luck would shine on an engaged couple for the rest of their lives. A special symbolic representation used for newly married couples was that of the Greek letters Alpha and Omega (the beginning and the end) surrounded by a garter and accompanied by a number of love messages. These particular items were worn close to the heart as it was believed they would give protection from adultery and other marital problems.

However, this cosy picture of a local witch giving hope and blessings to local residents is only one side of the story, because Molly Milburn appears to have also had a dark side to her character. It is recorded that on 5 October 1663, she appeared before local magistrates charged with publicly cursing local farmers and enchanting their cows so that 'a grevious scab dyd break out amang them'. She was found guilty of 'working great evil' and was sentenced to be publicly whipped for her transgressions.

Nanny Howe of Kildale was another wily old crone who had a credible reputation with local residents, including, it was believed, the power to expel the Devil, who had allegedly caused cattle diseases and other problems on local farms. On one occasion, she claimed she had climbed aboard her broomstick and flown across the Yorkshire Moors in close pursuit of Old Nick, later asking local residents for a coin to buy ingredients to make up a new batch of her magic flying mix. When the sceptical residents asked why she had not apprehended the Devil in the first place, Nanny told them that just as she was about to grab him, one of his black imps had jumped on her broomstick, dragging it to one side and disrupting her flight path. The extra weight had also caused her to land in a clump of trees and so ended the pursuit. Incredible as it may seem, the gullible listeners were quite happy with the witch's explanation as to how the wily old Devil had escaped her clutches and gladly donated a coin each (to Nanny Howe's obvious delight).

Finally, though known as the Pickering Witch to those who lived further afield, we have the witch whose common name amongst Whitby householders was 'Old Nanny'. She has the reputation of being one of the last witches to actually practice her craft in the Whitby district. History does not record her name, but we do know that she was a widow who lived in a remote location called Rawcliffe Woods at Levisham. In the late 1800s she had a formidable reputation for being skilled in all aspects of the Black Arts and used some peculiar devices in her spells including a 'destiny-telling garter', 'magic cubes' and discs and parchments carrying mystical images. A Whitby man, Shaw Jeffrey, writing about Old Nanny said that he had been in correspondence with a person who had actually met the woman when she, the correspondent, had stayed in a nearby farm as a child. Despite the warnings of the farmer and his wife that they would be bewitched if they went anywhere near Old Nanny, the girl and her family had decided to satisfy their curiosity and to go and see the notorious old crone for themselves. The correspondent dispelled any myths about the feared old woman, saying, 'I can remember as a child staying at Levisham, in the eighties, and my father and mother going to see her. They found her a very harmless old crone and bought a corner cupboard and delft plate rack from her.'

Little is known about Hester Dale, though we know she was a real person. Locals believed she was a shape-shifter, a witch who was able to turn herself into any animal shape she desired. Farmers attending Whitby market constantly related tales of how she had appeared to them on the way to market in the form of a wild or domestic animal. Hester lived in the mid-1750s and was credited with being able to cause animals, especially horses and donkeys, to become motionless. A single story survives of her supposed demonic talents. It has been repeatedly told over many years by Robert George Tinbull of Marske and his descendants. Old Robert Tinbull's horses had once become frozen by Hester Dale whilst crossing a reputedly haunted old stone bridge near Redcar (the date of the incident is given specifically in one account, namely the evening of Friday 9 September 1757). It is said that whilst crossing the bridge, Tinbull's horses refused to go either forward or backwards, despite assistance from a number of passers-by who pulled and tugged at the horses' reins. After an hour of trying to shift the horses, one of these men, Tom Wilson, suggested that the animals may have been 'spelled' by Hester Dale. Tinbull agreed that this was possible, saying that he had had a number of 'run-ins' with her recently on the way to Whitby market.

The horses were by now causing a traffic jam on the bridge. Suddenly, Tom Wilson said he had an idea, and without further ado, he rushed off into the distance. He returned almost immediately carrying a branch from a Rowan tree, a red-berried tree that had long been associated with having adverse affects on witches. The men struck the horses repeatedly with the swatch of leaves and berries, and instantly they began to move forward, to a cheer from a group of boys and men who had gathered at the bridge to lend assistance. No one now had any reservations in believing that the horses had been frozen by a magic spell. Their suspicions were immediately confirmed when, at the moment the horses began to move, a startled black cat ran across the road near the bridge and vanished into the undergrowth nearby. The gathering crowd was in no doubt that the only person in the district who could cast horse-freezing spells and shift her shape into a black cat was Hester Dale. Consequently, an official complaint was made against the woman to the local magistrate.

Another witch who gained a reputation for being a shape-shifter was Mary Nares whose regular appearance on the roadside is said to have terrified the travellers carrying sea salt from Saltwick salt-pans to Pickering via Saltersgate (not Saltergate, as the modern road-sign makers have mistakenly renamed it). If local superstition is to be believed, Mary could change herself from a hare to a dog and then to a frog in the blink of an eye. She was also famed for her 'hanging spells' which she sold to the gullible public. These were designed to be hung around the neck of those about to give birth and it is possible that, like many village witches, she acted as a midwife when children were born in her own locality.

CHAPTER EIGHT

The Goths Are Coming!

A Look at the Town's Modern Gothic Community

Whitby Goth Weekend is a paradise for all who are seduced by vampires, fantasy, darkness and mystery... The majority wear fascinating and unique black costumes and dramatic make up, and the public houses overspill with captivating dark characters.

(Bats & Broomsticks Guest House)

Whitby has been called the Goth Capital of Britain, and there is no doubt that those drawn to the modern Gothic lifestyle feel at home here. Crowds of exquisitely dressed people gather for the regular Gothic gatherings, and couples stay overnight or stop for a weekend break throughout the year – in the full knowledge that their sense of dress is accepted as completely normal by the people of the town.

Non-residents are sometimes taken aback by the unexpected sight of women with whitened faces or men dressed in kilts and stockings wearing top hats, but in Whitby this passes as normal. Tourists often return home after staying here during a Goth festival with tales of the strange dress of the Whitby population, totally unaware they have witnessed a special event and that the majority of Whitby's townsfolk never dress this way at all. After the festival, Whitby's Gothic visitors return home to occupations ranging from doctors, lawyers and airline pilots to milkmen, builders and shop assistants.

Specialist shops have now begun to open to cater for the fashions of local and visiting Goths. More unusual is this Gothic guest house with its sumptuous Victorian décor and its selection of Gothic memorabilia waiting to greet visitors at the door.

Origins

Whitby's Gothic festivals have grown from humble beginnings to become some of the most popular Gothically themed events in existence, attracting lovers of everything dark and mysterious from across the UK – and even from around the world. Men, women and children gather in the town to 'strut their stuff', often in outrageous and sometimes revealing costumes or wearing fascinating and often expensively tailored period costumes. In their dramatic make-up, they dance the night away at the local Spa and Metropole Hotel or simply chat with friends at one of the over-spilling pubs whose signs – 'Goths Welcome' – echo the feeling of the local population. The themed events were dreamed up by the local organiser, Jo Hampshire. She originally contacted around forty pen pals and came up with the idea for a gathering of like-minded individuals in 1994. They chose Whitby as the first event's venue because of its Dracula connections, and also because of the town's non-judgemental and welcoming atmosphere, which probably stems from the very earliest times when strangely dressed sailors and individuals from many lands would arrive in Whitby Harbour to load up with supplies before continuing on their way.

At first the Goth Festival was a yearly event, but because of its popularity the main gathering now takes place twice yearly (in April and October). Thousands of Goths descend upon the town and fill its streets (though the town's Gothic associations have become so well known that Goths also visit the area throughout the year). During the festivals, holiday accommodation is at a premium, boarding houses, hotels and holiday flats are crammed to the seams with black-costumed enthusiasts. Those that are particularly lucky and book well in advance may secure a place at the unique Bats & Broomsticks guesthouse with its stylish Victorian bedrooms and interior; its outside is also unique, bedecked with images of griffins, green men, devils, sun symbols and even Count Dracula himself.

What is a Goth?

Many, including the Goths themselves, have struggled with defining what a Goth actually is. Superficially, they can be identified usually, but not always, by their black clothing, black hair, and dark eye make-up. Others have whitened faces and typically wear outrageous or revealing costumes. Some are interested in vampires, mysticism and all things dark, but it must be said that such interests are all in the 'nicest possible taste'. During festivals, Whitby finds its streets and byways full of women in black lipstick competing for space with long-haired gents in cloaks and top hats carrying silver walking canes. Men in skirts and fishnet tights jostle for position with people of both sexes wearing a variety of appendages ranging from angel's wings to Devil's tails.

The festival's organiser, Jo Hampshire, is quoted as saying, 'It's said that if you play the A side of 'Spiceworld' whilst watching a third generation copy of 'Wake' with the sound turned down, the true meaning of Goth is revealed!' Jo, whose commendable drive to make the Goth Weekends an ever-increasing success, also reveals, 'I do have a strange affinity with Dorothy [of Wizard of Oz fame]... like her I started out in the middle of a black and white small-town mentality and my curiosity sent me tumbling into a weird and colourful world where things were never the same again.'

If defining a Goth proves difficult, describing the Goth Week festivities is equally tricky. Though many 'uninitiated' observers expect black magic

Hearses, skulls and skeletons are part of the local scene during Goth Week. Though most Goths arrive by car, bus or train, a few enter the town in their own macabre vehicles.

rituals, nothing could be further from the truth. Most of Whitby's visitors spend their time doing what 'normal' individuals do on holiday: dancing, eating candy floss, listening to music, drinking in pubs, placing a bet at the bookies, visiting the amusement arcades, taking their children for a hamburger or a bag of chips, or simply mixing with friends old and new at the annual Bizarre Bazaar.

Like the Edinburgh Festival, the Goth Festival has begun to expand to accommodate fringe events in local hotels and other venues, such as Dead Funny, a night of stand-up comedy specially formulated for a Gothic audience. Musical events are also popular and have attracted some odd-sounding performers including: Inkubus Sukkubus; Nekromantik; The Faces Of Sarah; Alien_Sex_Fiend; Zombina and The Skeletones; and Sheep_on_Drugs.

If proof were needed that the crowds of Goths that attend these events are caring people, one has only to look at their fund-raising event following the

Goth festivities are for all the family, and youngsters enjoy the celebrations as much as their parents.

murder of Sophie Lancaster. Sophie was tragically killed in a mob attack by teenagers at Stubbylee Park, Bacup near Rossendale in Lancashire in 2007, simply because she was wearing Gothic clothing. Her boyfriend narrowly escaped death in the same vicious attack. A stall held by the Gothic community in Whitby's Spa Pavilion sold small black ribbon roses in Sophie's memory and provided a memorial bench on the West Cliff in January 2008. The bench

Where else could a woman in a Gothic black outfit be seen accompanying a kilted man in traditional Scottish wear? But in Whitby it's normal – anything goes!

stands close to the Royal Hotel where Bram Stoker stayed on some of his later visits to Whitby.

Charity is never far from the hearts of the Gothic community, and other charitable events have included a football match between the Goths and a team from the local *Whitby Gazette* newspaper, a 'Dunk the Witch' evening dip in the sea and a night containing a strange blend of Goth, alternative and electronic body music mixed with more traditional 1980s favourites.

These two fashionable Goths prove that whether you go for big hair or a minimalist cut, no one cares – as long as it looks good and you are enjoying yourself!

It will surprise lots of people to find that, contrary to popular belief, a number of Goths are practicing Christians who attend church on Sundays. Others will spend Sundays taking quiet walks along the beach with their families or strolling along Whitby's coastline. If you should come across them and have your camera handy, don't be afraid to approach them for a photograph: most will relish the attention that their costumes attract and will gladly pose for photographers.

If you're coming to the Goth Festival, be sure to bring a camera. Most Goths will relish the attention that their way-out costumes attract, and will gladly pose for photographers.

The atmosphere of Gothic romance is never far from the surface and some have actually taken their wedding vows in the town. In October 2007 St Mary's parish church was the venue for the renewal of vows for two married Goths, Tony and Angela of Stockton-On-Tees. The bride and groom were dressed in full Gothic outfits, as were their band of guests.

No less an authority than *The Times* newspaper has shown an interest in Whitby's Gothic culture. In an article on Saturday 26 April 2008, under the headline 'Whitby Gothic Weekend is a lesson in British tolerance', Richard Morrison made comments on the gatherings of Goths in the town. His praise for the tolerance of the residents of Whitby people provides a particularly fitting end to this book:

And finally...
variety is the spice
of life, and despite
the vast range
of costumes,
everyone fits in.

They are an endearing bunch. In spite of their strenuous efforts to project themselves as Satanic ghouls, corpse-botherers and insatiable transsexual deviants, it's quite clear that none would harm a fly... We talk a lot, usually disapprovingly, about 'tribal mentality'. But after 50,000 years it's probably too deeply ingrained in the human psyche to be erased. Instead, we should be encouraging young people to gravitate to tribes that bring joy to themselves without harming or antagonising others. The Whitby Gothic Weekend is the epitome of that. The Goths have fun and supply a bizarre three-day fashion parade. The townsfolk smile benignly, and the pubs do a roaring trade. That's Britain at its tolerant best!

Bibliography and Further Reading

Aubrey, John, *Remaines of Gentilisme and Judaisme*, (orig. 1686), W. Satchell, Peyton, London (1881)

Barrington, Edward, *Annals of the House of Percy, from the Conquest to the opening of the Nineteenth Century*, Richard Clay & Sons (1887)

Brenan, Gerald, *A History of the House of Percy From the Earliest Times Down to the Present Century, Vol. I*, Freemantle, London (1902)

Burton, Janet, *The Monastic Order in Yorkshire, 1069-1215*, Cambridge University Press (1999)

Calendar of the Patent Rolls, Edward III, 1354-1374, His Majesty's Stationery Office (1909 / 1913 & 1914)

Charlton, Lionel, *A History of Whitby and of Whitby Abbey*, Ward (1779)

English Heritage, Whitby Abbey Headland Project, *Southern Anglian Enclosure Report, Update 2* (July 1999)

Feiling, Keith, *A History of England*, first published in 1950 and republished by Book Club Associates (1975)

Report on the fixtures and fittings at Bagdale Old Hall, Whitby, Giles Quarme & Associates, London (1997)

Henderson, William, *From Folklore of the Northern Counties*, W. Satchell, Peyton and Co. Covent Garden, London (1879)

Holt, Robert Burbank, *Whitby Past & Present*, Copas (1890)

Jeffrey, Shaw, *Whitby Lore & Legend*, Horne & Sons, Whitby (1923)

Kaempfer, Engelbert, *History of Japan*, James MacLehose and Sons, Glasgow (1906)

Lenkin, Edward J., *Picture Rocks – American Indian Rock Art in the Northeast Woodlands*, University Press of New England (2002)

Lindemann, Mary, *Medicine and Society in Early Modern Europe*, Cambridge University Press (1999)

Pantin, William Abel, ed. *Documents Illustrating the Activities of the General and Provincial Chapters of the English Black Monks, 1215-1540, Vol. iii* (1937)

Petrinovich, Lewis F., *The Cannibal Within*, Aldine De Gruyter (2000)

Poe, Edgar Allan, *Narrative of Arthur Gordon Pym*, Penguin Books Ltd (1975)

Richardson, John, *Local Historian's Encyclopedia*, Historical Publications (1975)

Ruskin, John, *The Stones of Venice*, J.M. Dent & Sons (1921)

Tatarkiewicz, Wladyslaw, *History of Aesthetics*, Continuum International, New York (2006)

Thurrock Heritage Factfiles 19, 'Fangs for the Memory: The Purfleet Dracula Connection', Thurrock Council (2008)

Young, Revd. George, *A History of Whitby & Streoneshalh Abbey*, Clark & Medd, Whitby (1817)

Other titles published by The History Press

Whitby Then & Now: The Second Selection

COLIN WATERS

Whitby Then & Now reveals an on-going and ever shifting era of social change, illustrate
through fascinating pictures of long gone residents, fisher-folk, changing streets and
evolving buildings. The constant activity of the town's harbour and coastline is depicted
using images dating from Whitby's earliest days up to modern times. This absorbing
pictorial record provides a fascinating insight into the life of this bustling historic town
and is an essential addition to the bookshelf of any lover of historic Whitby.

978 0 7524 4657 8

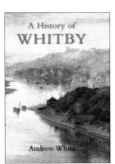

A History of Whitby

ANDREW WHITE

Largely derived from its unusual past, the town's unique character draws thousands of
visitors each year; and the first edition of this book, in 1993, was as much welcomed
by them as by the locals. The only comprehensive history of Whitby, it rapidly sold out
and Dr White, its author, of ancient Whitby stock, has now fully revised and updated hi
book, with some new illustrations and interpretations. This new edition will continue a
the definitive work on the town, as well as a very entertaining story.

978 1 8607 7306 8

Haunted Whitby

ALAN BROOKE

The ruins of Whitby Abbey provide an ideal setting for ghost stories. Many ghostly
experiences in the abbey grounds feature here, including an account of treasure hunters
who were in search of rich pickings and were disturbed by an unimpressed spectre. The
town is perhaps best-known as one of the locations for Bram Stoker's Dracula. With storie
of haunted lighthouses, the strange apparitions of Bagdale Hall and the spirit of Nunningt
Hall, *Haunted Whitby* is a must-read for anyone interested in the town's paranormal past.

978 0 7524 4925 8

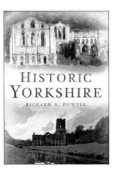

Historic Yorkshire

RICHARD A. POWELL

This volume celebrates every aspect of Yorkshire's history. Including subjects as diverse
as Roman Yorkshire, Yorkshire castles and abbeys, historic York and coaching days in
Yorkshire, prehistoric Yorkshire, Yorkshire folklore, Robin Hood of Yorkshire, ghost
houses, and industry, canals and railways, it is a fascinating tour through Yorkshire's past.
Richly illustrated and meticulously researched, this book will delight all lovers of the
Dales.

978 0 7524 4926 5

Visit our website and discover thousands of other History Press books.

www.thehistorypress.co.uk